LITERARY DOGS & THEIR SOUTH CAROLINA WRITERS

HUB CITY
PRESS

SPARTANBURG SC · 2012

LITERARY DOGS
& THEIR SOUTH CAROLINA WRITERS

EDITED BY JOHN LANE AND BETSY WAKEFIELD TETER

This project is supported in part by an award from the National Endowment for the Arts.

ART WORKS.

arts.gov

First printing, November 2012
Book design: Brandy Lindsey and The Graphics House Inc.
Cover photo: Avery Locklear (imagebyavery.com)
Proofreaders: Vanessa Lucas, Jan Scalisi, and Sarah Miles Westberry
Printed in Saline, MI by McNaughton & Gunn Inc.

"A Manifesto for Pet Cremation" by George Singleton previously appeared in Garden & Gun magazine. Roger Pinckney gratefully acknowledges prior publication of "Zebo" in Sporting Classics magazine.

Photography: Tommy Hays's Emily was shot by Michael Mauney. All photographs of Josephine Humphreys and Archie were taken by Avery Locklear, age 17. The author photo of Dorothea Benton Frank was taken by Debbie Zammit; Marshall Chapman by Anthony Scarlati; Padgett Powell by Gately Williams; Marjory Wentworth by Karen Donner; Tommy Hays by Michael Mauney; Glenis Redmond by Daniel Perales; Chaser portrait by Mark Olencki; dog image on page 81, Bill Del-Sette.

Literary dogs & their South Carolina writers / John Lane & Betsy Wakefield Teter, editors.
    p. cm.
ISBN 978-1-891885-98-3 (alk. paper)
1. American literature–South Carolina. 2. Dog owners–South Carolina–Anecdotes. 3. Authors, American–South Carolina--Anecdotes. 4. Dogs–South Carolina--Anecdotes. 5. Human-animal relationships–South Carolina. I. Lane, John, 1954- II. Teter, Betsy Wakefield.
PS266.S6L58 2013
810.9'9757--dc23

2012026297

HUB CITY PRESS

186 W. Main St.
Spartanburg, SC 29306
864.577.9349
www.hubcity.org

In memory of Toby and Ellie Mae

Donors

The Hub City Writers Project thanks its friends who made contributions in support of this book and other Hub City programs:

Valerie and Bill Barnet
JM Smith Foundation
Marsha and Jimmy Gibbs
George Dean and Susu Johnson
Sara, Paul, and Ellis Lehner
Nathanial and Gayle Magruder
Jeanie and Patrick O'Shaughnessy
The Romill Foundation
The South Carolina Arts Commission
Sally and Warwick Spencer

Paula and Stan Baker
Colonial Trust Company
Elizabeth Fleming
Julian and Dorothy Josey
John Lane and Betsy Teter
Betty and Walter Montgomery
John and Stacy McBride
Dwight and Liz Patterson
White's Pine Street Exxon
Alanna and Don Wildman
Anne Marie and Dennis Wiseman

Arkwright Foundation
Mitch and Sarah Allen
Monta and Keith Anthony
Tom and Ceci Arthur
Robert and Susan Atkins
Vic and Lynn Bailey
Susan Baker
John and Isabel Barber
Jeff Barker
Tom and Joan Barnet
Marianne and Tom Bartram
Charles and Christi Bebko
Carol and Jim Bradof
Don and Martha Bramblett
John Moore and Susan Bridges
Bea Bruce
Nichole Buchanan
William W. Burns
Julia Burnett
Robert and Margaret Burnette
Kathy and Marvin Cann
Donna R. Cart
Robin Carter
Peter Caster
Randall and Sarah Chambers
Robert H. Chapman III
Nan and Tim Cleveland
Sally and Jerry Cogan
Rick and Sue Conner
Randall and Mary Lynn Conway
Paul and Nancy Coté
Tom Moore Craig
John and Kirsten Cribb
Betsy Cox and Mike Curtis
Mr. and Mrs. Magruder H. Dent

Paul and Tara Desmond
Chris and Alice Dorrance
Susan and James Dunlap
William C. Elston
Edwin Epps
Nick and Lisa Fleming
Steve and Abby Fowler
H. Laurence and Elizabeth Fritz
Caleb and Delie Fort
Ron and Melody Fulbright
Carol Young Gallagher
Joan Gibson
Ellen Goldey
Jan and Larry Goldstein
Barney and Elaine Gosnell
Jim and Kay Gross
Lee and Kitty Hagglund
Bob and Barbara Hammett
Tracy and Tom Hannah
Robert and Carolyn Harbison, III
John and Lou Ann Harrill, Jr.
Jonathan Haupt
Mike and Nancy Henderson
Peggy and David Henderson
Stephanie Highsmith
Susan Hodge
Charlie Hodge
Mr. and Mrs. J. Thomas Hollis
Myrta and David Holt
Mr. andMrs. Kenneth R. Huckaby
Woody and Carol Hughes
David and Harriet Ike
William A. James
Jinx Jenkins
Matt Johnson and Kim Rostan

Stewart and Ann Johnson
Wallace Eppes Johnson
Frannie Jordan
Elizabeth and Bill Joyce
Jay and Pam Kaplan
Angela Kelly
Bert and Ruth Knight
Janice and Wood Lay
Brandy Lindsey
George and Frances Loudon
Brownlee and Julie Lowry
Kelly Lowry and Rebecca Ramos
Robert and Nancy Lyon
Ed and Suzan Mabry
Zerno E. Martin, Jr.
Bill and Wendy Mayrose
John and Jill McBurney
Fayssoux McLean
Polly McTeer
Ed and Gail Medlin
Linda Merriman
Larry E. Milan
Boyce and Carole Miller
Robin Mizell
John and Belton Montgomery
John and Susan Murphy
Kam and Emily Neely
Elizabeth Nelson
Walter and Susan Novak
Jane and James Ovenden
Carolyn Pennell
Richard Pennell
Sarah Chambers and Becky Pennell
Mr. and Mrs. Edward P. Perrin
John and Lynne Poole

Philip and Frances Racine
Eileen Rampey
Karen Randall
Ron and Ann Rash
Allison and John Ratterree
Naomi Richardson
Andrew F. Rickis
Rose Mary Ritchie
Martial and Amy Robichaud
Gail Rodgers
Renee Romberger
Susan Schneider
George Singleton
Caroline and Ron Smith
Danny and Becky Smith
Lee and James Snell, Jr., Esq.
Betty B. Snow
Hank and Marla Steinberg
Tammy and David Stokes
George and Sissy Stone
Eliot and Michel Stone
Eric Svenson
Christine Swager
Nancy D. Taylor
Carol and Peter Theiler
Ray E. Thompson, Sr.
Bob and Cheryl Tillotson
Awakening Energies, Underwood
Mary Helen and Gregg Wade
Lawrence and Jerri Warren
David and Kathy Weir
Dave and Linda Whisnant
Karen and John B. White, Jr.
Cynthia and Stephen Wood
Bob and Carolyn Wynn

Preface

A stack of dog essays an inch thick sat on the big, black coffee table in our living room the cold January morning when Murphy began to have a little stomach trouble. The dog stories had been coming in for a month by email from a fine group of South Carolina writers. Novelists, poets, and journalists, now scattered across the world, sent us tales of Henry and Otto, Buckshot and Itch, Dooley and Universe. We knew it was time we start some serious editing for this book, *Literary Dogs & Their South Carolina Writers*, so it would be ready for its statewide launch in November.

Murphy, our overweight, short-legged beagle of indeterminate age, had other plans for the day. From his usual position on the living room couch, he raised his little platypus body, stiffened, and began that familiar arching of his back, moving the contents of his stomach outward through a series of rhythmic retching upchucks. You know how dogs throw up: one, *ugh*, two, *ugh*, three, *ugh*, then *BLEEGHHH*. We'd been through this drill many times, and it always sent us into a frenzy. We knew Murphy would move quickly toward the dining room rug, his favorite spot to let it go. The trick was to intercept him before he got there, sweep him up under an arm, head for the deck door, and let Murphy toss his cookies in a place that didn't require stain remover.

Before we could grab him at the couch, Murphy dropped to the hardwood floor, began his crouched serpentining across the room with us in pursuit, this time leaving a secret present of puke in the path to the deck door. In the chaos of chase, no one noticed. There was the frantic sound of dog toenails scraping across the floor, heavy human footsteps in one direction and then the other, a door flung open, and then AAAAAARRGGHH, whump!

Then this, an hour later, in the emergency room, after the ambulance and the stretcher and the flock of medical technicians:

Betsy: "How many people do you think are admitted to this emergency room for accidents involving dog vomit?"

John: "Mrrrrrpff." The intravenous drugs had obviously kicked in.

Dogs do this to people. They change things, and that's one of the reasons we wanted to gather these stories, to confirm in one place that just when you thought you understood the world, a dog enters and turns everything around. That doesn't *have* to mean two broken ribs, one in two places, and two weeks laid up in bed, but it does mean that we are often better people because of our dogs. (Murphy: "Look before you leap." Us: "Okay, we get it.") There's a scientific theory now that says we'd have never been fully human without domesticating the dog. The scientist who published this theory says that *Homo sapiens* had dogs with them when they wandered into frozen Europe and outfoxed their cousins, the Neanderthals. Dogs made us smarter.

And in this book we have some pretty smart people writing about memorable dogs. There are hunting dog stories from Roger Pinckney and Drew Lanham; old dog tales from Mark Powell, Nicole Seitz, and Dorothea Benton Frank; dog-versus-cat essays from Padgett Powell and Dot Jackson; and even the saga of a super-heroic pooch penned by Beth Webb Hart. There are tributes to long-gone dogs from Christopher Dickey, George Singleton, and Lou Dischler. Mary Alice Monroe, Tommy Hays, and Ron Rash relate stories of maniac canines (who have their good sides too). Glenis Redmond, Marshall Chapman, Janna McMahan, and Josephine Humphreys write about how dogs help bind them to their fathers. Beyond that, there's a whole kennel of rambunctious dog stories from Andrew Geyer, Mindy Friddle, Dinah Johnson, Marjory Wentworth, Elise Blackwell, Melinda Long, and Kate Salley Palmer.

Probably the most famous dog quotation brings together the two worlds we celebrate here: "Outside of a dog, a book is man's best friend. Inside of a dog it's too dark to read." Groucho Marx was fishing for a laugh, but we like to think that he was on to something. These pieces offer up some unexpected light. Settle on the couch and see where they take you—but watch out for the dog vomit!

John Lane
Betsy Wakefield Teter
June 2012

Table of Contents

Archie

Josephine Humphreys

I've owned and loved a lot of dogs in my life—
Andy, Baby, Gator, Ratzo, Zack, Toby, Ruby, Nelly,
Tater—but Archie is the dog of my old age, the one
I was waiting for. I catch myself talking to him as if
he were not a dog. "I'm going to the Piggly Wiggly,
but I'll be back in forty-five minutes. Do you need
anything?" Maybe this is a sign of my dotage. But
what is dotage if not that time of life when one's
allowed to dote? I'm a fool for the poodle. He came to
us at the right time.

Our children were long grown and gone. My
mother had just died after a hard disease, and my
father, ninety-five with Alzheimer's, had come to live
with me and my husband, Tom. We were all pretty
exhausted, and I found myself unable to write a whole
sentence. The future was something I couldn't think
about, and I was in denial about Alzheimer's. I told
myself Dad's memory might be shot through with
holes, but he was still himself, a gentle old-fashioned
man who hid his emotions the traditional Southern
way. My diagnosis was wear-and-tear compounded
by grief. He didn't talk about Mom. But one night
sitting alone on the screened porch he said, "Martha,
look at that moon!" and then almost in a whisper,
"Remember the day I asked you to marry me?"

It scared me to overhear that. Maybe he really

"I like to write when Archie's with me,
watching me do this curious thing. He's a
quiet presence, another consciousness in
the room. He doesn't understand what I'm
doing, but neither do I."

had lost touch with reality. But I resolved to stick to my diagnosis. Loss of true love is a surgery without anesthesia and will throw you into shock. The remedies that occurred to me seemed pathetic and meager. Find some old John Wayne movies, cook okra his favorite way, get him a dog? I tried them all.

"Dad, I found a dog on Craigslist for free. Let's go look at it. It's a big white poodle, a rescue dog.

"Rescue dog?"

"From the rescue shelter. His owner died in a car wreck. Other people are coming to look at him too. We have to get there first."

In the car he buckled his seatbelt and said, "Where did you say we're going?"

"To get a loyal companion," I said.

In the rescue-lady's living room Dad sat on the sofa with his hands on his knees. The poodle came in, the most beautiful dog I'd ever seen, and trotted straight to me. He was only eight months old, but he was friendly, he was curious, and for some reason I felt sure he was wise. The rescue-lady said he'd lived on a goat farm with his black twin, and the two dogs liked to play all day in the muddy goat-farm pond. When the farmer died they were sent to different foster homes to await adoption. And that was all she could tell us.

"Daddy, this dog's perfect for you."

"I don't like him."

"Why not?"

"He looks too much like a poodle."

"He is a poodle."

"I don't want one."

I didn't need to ask why. He'd be thinking a poodle's a French dog, a silly dog, not a manly man's dog like a Labrador.

I told the lady, "We'll take him."

Dad frowned.

"For me," I said. "I want him for me."

Adoption entails mystery. All my previous dogs were open books, but this one's story was murky. I tried to reconstruct it from clues. The day we got him, he balked at getting into the car. Don't all dogs love to ride in cars? But we had to wrestle him in. That's when it occurred to me that he might have been IN that wreck that killed his owner. So every night I carried his bowl of food out to the car and lured him in, fed him by hand in the back seat. After three days he was leaping in whenever we opened the door.

Other quirks were equally disturbing in their implications. Archie turned out to be afraid of brooms, and he wouldn't come near his food until after I had stepped clear away from it. Yet he was food-driven and would do anything for a treat. I envisioned a burly goat-farmer who skimped on Purina and swatted the dogs away with a broom if they tried to eat before the bowl was filled. I worried: might a traumatic childhood have damaged this dog in ways I could never cure? Although he wouldn't let me out of his sight for more than a minute, he wasn't cuddly. He would sleep at my feet but not at my side, and if I put my head down close to him when he was dozing, he growled. He didn't seem to warm up to men, preferring women. Maybe the goat-farmer's wife had slipped him some treats now and then.

But he was so smart, I figured I could teach him both tricks and trust. The tricks came easy. It took only minutes to teach him *sit, stay, shake, lie down, fetch. Jump through the hula hoop* took five minutes, and *roll over* about ten. *Jump the broom* was tougher. We played with the broom first, and I patted it. Nice broom, friendly broom. He stepped over it, and then I raised it an inch off the floor, and he stepped again, and pretty soon he was happily jumping three feet high to clear the no-longer-dreaded broom.

We settled into happy patterns. Archie agreed to go fishing with Tom and became a regular at the tackle shop and the hardware store. People stared at the poodle riding in the beat-up Jeep with his head out the window just like the Labs in other Jeeps, or leaning into the wind at the bow of the motorboat, ears flying wide. Once when I was walking him, a big black SUV pulled up, and the driver, a Russian tourist, rolled down his tinted window to ask if his children could have their pictures taken with "the animal." Another day a Latino man stopped me and pointed to Archie: "*Perro o oveja?*" "Dog or sheep?"

Still, during those first few weeks I detected a sadness in the poodle's eyes, something not all that different from what I saw in my father and felt in myself. Not a day went by that I didn't automatically reach for the phone to call my mother. That particular loss, the cut-off of communication, was the hardest for me, and I was unable to summon her up the way my father could. I tried but could not say, "Come look at the moon."

Archie was the first to begin to mend. He revealed a maternal instinct, taking his stuffed animals to bed with him, cleaning their ears, licking them clean. He developed an eager affection for the dolphins that followed the motorboat, for the dogs at the dog park, for Tom and Dad and my sister and the helpers who come to sit with Dad. One day our neighbors got a new dog and brought her over to meet ours, and when Archie saw Emmylou, he froze in his tracks. Suddenly he went crazy, zooming in circles and lunging at her in canine ecstasy, as if she were a long lost sweetheart. I understood: she was a big black poodle. Nuzzling, romping, licking, he must have rejoiced, at some deep level of his brain, at the recovery of his twin. Now two years later Emmylou is still his obsession. Their favorite play is to leap into the muddy marsh together, and even when she's not around he looks for her.

I don't know how to tell about the rest of us. Somehow we were lifted by this dog's joy, by his weird dignity, his careful listening, and his attention to us.

Tom calls him a keen observer of human behavior—always watching our patterns, interpreting our moves, and increasingly, learning our language. We've taken to spelling out words (like "Emmylou" and "squirrel") and even whole sentences ("Someone's coming") to avert that canine ecstasy he's prone to, and the alter-ego we call Crazy Dog.

After I explained to Dad that poodles originated as hunting retrievers, "puddle-hounds," he grew more enthusiastic about Archie. He delights in the poodle now, especially the tricks. We've stopped giving him the Alzheimer's medication, and the neurologist has said he doesn't need to see Dad any more. I don't mean that the poodle was a cure for that terrible disease; I have no idea why it seemed to go away, or at least halt in its progress. But I do believe that the rescue dog rescued us, reconnected us to the world and me to words. I like to write when Archie's with me, watching me do this curious thing. He's a quiet presence, another consciousness in the room. He doesn't understand what I'm doing, but neither do I. And we both accept that. Hopeful befuddlement is the ideal state of mind for a dog and for a writer.

One night last week he was playing with his tennis ball. He'll dribble it, dropping it and catching it on the bounce, then toss it and fetch it for himself. This time he rolled the ball to an unreachable spot under the bookcase, then sat in front of Tom and waited. Tom got the ball out and returned it to Archie, who then nudged it under the bookcase again and looked to Tom for help.

"You don't learn, do you," Tom said, once more getting the ball out.

"Oh, he learns," I said. "He just learned how to teach you to fetch."

And I have a feeling there's more to learn from the big white rescue dog.

Josephine Humphreys is a native of Charleston, and the author of four novels, most recently *Nowhere Else on Earth*. She has won a Guggenheim Fellowship and a Literature Award from the American Academy of Arts and Letters. Currently she lives on Sullivan's Island with her husband, Tom Hutcheson, and Archie.

Adventures with Seamus Heaney and My Mother-in-Law

Andrew Geyer

This is not a mother-in-law story. This is a story about a dog, a little girl, and a modern-day American family that's a lot more like the Brady Bunch than Ozzie and Harriet. But my mother-in-law does figure prominently in the working-out of the plot.

The dog's name is Seamus Heaney, after my second favorite poet. And he is my dog, I guess, if it can truly be said that a dog "belongs" to anyone. It's probably more accurate to say that I am his person. Seamus Heaney didn't start out to be my dog, but we'll get to that part of the story later.

The little girl's name is Savannah. Savannah is my stepdaughter, and she is lovely: pale-skinned, strawberry-blonde, a miniature version of her mother, Emily. Emily is the love of my life. Joshua and Caleb are the other members of our modern-day Brady Bunch. They are my sons, Emily's stepsons, Savannah's stepbrothers. Both of them love Seamus Heaney in the rough-and-tumble way that boys love dogs. But as they are only with us during the summer, on holidays, and on occasional weekends, the primary supporting characters in the story of Seamus the dog are Savannah, Emily, and myself.

"If saying that Seamus Heaney has become an integral part of our modern-day Brady Bunch family means admitting that my mother-in-law was right, so be it."

As for my mother-in-law …

Well, my mother-in-law is the reason that Seamus Heaney (the dog, not his Nobel-winning namesake) made the 700-mile journey from an art colony in Arkansas to live in the 118-year-old house that Emily and I are slowly renovating in Graniteville, South Carolina. Despite Emily's and my adamant refusal—I believe I actually used the words "over my dead body"—my mother-in-law was absolutely determined that her granddaughter have a dog.

We should probably pause to reflect a moment on why one might choose to name a Welsh Border Collie after an Irish poet. Our orange tabby housecat, Charles Dickens, might well answer: Why not? But there are several reasons that I think are pretty good, not the least of which is my German-Irish heritage. My father comes from a family of no-nonsense German landowners, while my mother is descended from a brood of wild-eyed Irish ne'er-do-wells. Even more important is the fact that—like his Irish poet namesake—one of Seamus the dog's best things is "Digging." This is particularly the case when Seamus the dog feels that he has not been played fetch with enough by me (obviously still breathing despite losing the dog battle with my mother-in-law) or rough-and-tumbled with enough by Joshua and Caleb. And like all great poets, Welsh Border Collies are wicked smart when it comes to language. There is a recorded case of a Border collie in Spartanburg who knows, and responds to, more than one thousand words of the Queen's English. Seamus the dog's favorite words include "fetch," "squeaky" (a beloved chew-toy that makes a high-pitched squeal when bitten), "outside," "peanut butter," "bone," "wrestle," and "go." His least favorite word is "no."

To be honest, the word "fetch" has also become a favorite of mine. It turns out that there is no better therapy, when the stress level of our Brady Bunch life rises to a fever pitch, than throwing a slobbery tennis ball to a black-and-white-and-brown streak of a dog whose eyes are afire with the pure joy of running. But I digress.

While the word "no" works wonders with Seamus the dog, it has turned out to be less effective when it comes to my mother-in-law. My mother-in-law is nothing if not determined. A regionally prominent artist whose paintings grace the walls of Emily's and my Graniteville home, along with the walls of art galleries and a great many other homes throughout the South, my mother-in-law has achieved excellence in her *métier* through the combination of talent and single-minded intensity that all great artists (including Irish poets laureate) share. It was at an art colony that my mother-in-law introduced Savannah to the black-and-white-and-brown puppy who would eventually be named Seamus Heaney. To help pay the bills, the art colony does double-duty as a working plant nursery and registered Welsh Border Collie farm.

In addition to her mother's classic beauty,

Savannah shares her grandmother's considerable artistic talent. And over the course of one summer, between lessons at the art colony in Arkansas where her grandmother was teaching, Savannah became acquainted with a certain tiny, fuzzy, black-and-white-and-brown puppy who had not been born with his brothers' and sisters' perfect markings. Make no mistake: Seamus the dog is the scion of not one but two noble (and hence shockingly high-dollar) lines of work and show dogs. If not for the accident of his imperfect coloration, he would have been far beyond the modest means of a university professor and a high school English teacher. This fact, relayed through the (then) seven-year-old Savannah, played a key role in my mother-in-law's strategy.

"Mama," little Savannah said over the phone to Emily one morning in July, "can I have a dog? One of the puppies here has fallen in love with me."

"Oh, honey," Emily said, "we could never afford one of those puppies. And besides, what would Charles Dickens say?"

"We could afford this one. My grandma says that he's not perfect like the other puppies, so he only costs a hundred dollars."

"Savannah? Would you please put your grandmother on the phone?"

The ensuing long-distance difference of opinion included less-than-pleasant moments that I'll not recount here. Relevant details include some admittedly ungenerous comments from a ranch-raised husband (I grew up on a working cattle ranch in Southwest Texas where, with the exception of a spoiled indoor cat—my no-nonsense German father's grudging concession to my very determined Irish mother—four-legged animals lived outside, and the only animals that ate were those that worked); assorted objections from a practical wife who foresaw the difficulties a dog would add to the already-complicated holiday travel arrangements of a modern-day Brady Bunch family; and a grandmother whose sole concern was the fact that her granddaughter had fallen in love with a certain black-and-white-and-brown Border Collie puppy. The tear-choked promises of that same dog-besotted granddaughter to feed said dog, wash said dog, and play with said dog every day figured prominently in each conversational pause.

Has a pair of practical and well-meaning, but heart-crushingly loving, parents ever won an argument like this one?

Strangely, in this case, I believe the answer is yes. Of course, Seamus Heaney (the dog) came to live in South Carolina. And of course, Savannah's tear-choked promises about dog care were fulfilled only for about the usual term of such desperate and emotion-fueled oaths. The duties of daily dog maintenance devolved upon Emily and me—Emily took over the dog-washing chore; the feeding, watering, and playing-with responsibilities are now mine. But in my humble opinion, having taken a couple of years now to consider, these details are beside the point.

In his Nobel Lecture, Seamus Heaney (the Irish poet) said that as "writers and readers, as sinners and citizens, our realism and our aesthetic sense make us wary of crediting the positive note." With all due deference to the great poet and Nobel laureate, this has not been the case with Seamus the dog and me. Over the course of my newfound dog duties, I have become—to my great surprise—even more besotted with a certain black-and-white-and-brown Border Collie than Savannah ever thought about being. And I am happy to report that my love has been returned a thousandfold. Literally.

For both Seamus the dog and myself, the most positive note in our relationship has been our daily game of fetch. Every afternoon, I walk in the front door and set down my briefcase; Seamus bounds to the back door, where he proceeds to bounce up and down; and I follow, pausing only to take a tennis ball from the dog pantry before we head into the back yard. Then I throw, and he fetches, over and over and over again. He has trained me well. His favorite thing is for me to throw the ball up high, so that it ricochets off the close-cut carpet grass—and Seamus leaps after it, snatching the yellow missile out of the air. The slobbery testament of his affection coats my fingers and palms like a glove; and the stresses of university professorship, holiday travel arrangements, and renovating a 118-year-old house fade away.

If saying that Seamus Heaney has become an integral part of our modern-day Brady Bunch family means admitting that my mother-in-law was right, so be it. In the broadest, most positive sense, we are all winners here: Savannah, Joshua and Caleb, Emily and myself, and of course Seamus the dog.

The only real loser, I guess, is our orange tabby housecat, Charles Dickens—who has not exactly grown to love our family's newest addition. But that is another story.

Andrew Geyer's books are *Dixie Fish*, a novel; *Siren Songs from the Heart of Austin*, a story cycle; *Meeting the Dead*, a novel; and *Whispers in Dust and Bone*, a story cycle that won the silver medal in the *Foreword Magazine* book of the year awards and a Spur Award from the Western Writers of America. His award-winning short stories have appeared in dozens of literary magazines and anthologies, and been nominated for the Pushcart Prize. A member of the Texas Institute of Letters, he currently serves on the creative writing faculty at the University of South Carolina Aiken.

Henry Frank –
Dog Extraordinaire

Dorothea Benton Frank

Life as I knew it ceased to exist with the birth of my daughter. Then along came my son. Everyone with children will tell you that once you have children you may as well get pets because your partying days are over, done, finished, *kaput*. So I surrendered my career, relocated to the suburbs of New Jersey, learned to drive the turnpike with maniacs to the left, right, ahead and behind of my wholly unglamorous minivan, reprogrammed my brain and dove headlong (how else?) into the business of raising children. Several years of sandbox play dates, birthday parties with clowns and magicians, zoo visits, forts and castles made of cardboard boxes, visits from Santa and the Tooth Fairy passed, and yet, something was missing. Pets, we decided. Yes, we needed a pet.

We tried fish. A long series of them, all named Bill, grew to a certain size, and before I could do anything about acquiring a larger tank, they flew into the air, landed on the carpet and expired. My son, three at the time, said they committed "sewercide," and I couldn't really blame them. Circumnavigating that same little tank day in and day out had to be mind-numbingly depressing. And for us, all those goldfish named Bill were seriously less than emotionally satisfying.

Next, we had a brief encounter with a terrorist

"A dog psychic once told me I had to stop telling Henry I was going to the store for milk when I was really going on book tour for weeks."

kitten named Phoebe who only wanted to scratch, hiss, and hang from the top of my curtains. She frightened us all; *all* includes my long-suffering husband whose eyes darted around the room before entering. "Just wanted to say hello to Phoebe," he would lie. We quickly found her a more compatible situation.

With Phoebe out of the picture a new campaign, a withering one, was born. My children wanted a dog. A puppy. Something they could grow up with, love and cherish. A dog would give them a certain responsibility, they argued. They would do all the work. I wouldn't have to do a thing. If I would just buy the food and pay for the vet, they'd see about the puppy's meals, exercise, and emotional needs. Naturally, even with the few brain cells I had left, I recognized this scheme as a snare and a delusion. But I gave in because truthfully, I sort of wanted a puppy too. So the search began.

It was the era of Pre-Google and I'm not quite sure how I researched different breeds but we finally settled on a relative newcomer to the AKC pantheon of pups and began to seek a breeder of Cavalier King Charles Spaniels, known for their gentle spirit and love of companionship. Of course the best one we could find was hours and hours away by car, in the hinterland of Pennsylvania.

I telephoned the breeder who told me she was expecting a litter in a few weeks and why didn't I drive over with the children when the puppies were born to see if there was one we might be interested in having after it was weaned. I realized then that this would be a process, an interview really, to determine whether or not we were trustworthy enough to adopt one of her baby Cavaliers. Would our minivan impress her? Probably not. Would my children poison it with chocolate, feed it Legos, neglect or harm it in any way? I surely hoped not. To be completely honest, my son Will at now four years of age was afraid of the most docile canine, including those operated with batteries. Anything that yipped, licked, or jumped sent him into a frenzied state. So I began to make up stories about Cavaliers and how wonderful it was going to be to have a little dog in our life, hoping to assuage Will's anxiety and to give him and Victoria, who was seven, everything to look forward to and little to doubt. We drove to Pennsylvania as soon as we could after the litter arrived.

Seven four-week-old pink bellied puppies, falling down, tumbling over each other, sleepy eyed babies awaited this breathless-with-excitement trio. We were in love with them all. But six had been chosen by other families, and that left us the tiniest creature, the literal runt of the litter. We didn't care. We loved him. He was going to be ours. We were going to be his. And as soon as we could, we brought him home and named him Henry. He proved to be a brilliant choice. He was so smart he could practically read our minds. There was only one problem with Henry; there wasn't enough of him to go around. Everyone wanted to hold him. Everyone wanted to play with him. Everyone wanted him in their bed, except my husband who said there would NEVER be a dog in his bed. So naturally, we went back to Pennsylvania on the arrival of the next litter.

Buster Brown was Henry's second cousin. Buster was absolutely adorable and had the same coloring and markings as Henry. He was not as cerebral as Henry—he was just all dog. Poor Henry was devastated, betrayed that we loved another dog, and he hated Buster on sight. But Buster persevered and somehow these famously companionable dogs found their groove.

Over the next twelve years we witnessed bouts of competition for the Alpha Dog title between them, but when it got drafty in the kitchen, they snuggled up together to stay warm. We mistook this for friendship or a truce. It wasn't until Buster went to doggie heaven three years ago that Henry got happy again. I was heartbroken from our loss and appalled by Henry's behavior. Henry became a born-again puppy. He's fourteen now and shows little to no sign of aging. I should change his name to Magic because according to the breed's actuarial tables, he was supposed to be singing with the Hallelujah chorus a while back but no, Henry's gonna live forever. I hope. Because what we've all come to understand at the deepest level is that we can't bear the thought of living without him.

After the children left for college and adulthood, Henry, the formerly cranky, jealous, complicated, territorial Henry, who always had a worried look on his face as though we were bringing home another dog any minute to ruin his life, became my shadow. He lives on my heels and has even figured out how to open the bathroom door, which goes without saying, is too much for me.

All he has to do is see me with a suitcase and he spirals down into a moody funk. A dog psychic once told me I had to stop telling Henry I was going to the store for milk when I was really going on book tour for weeks. Hen sat there with an expression of self-righteous indignation as if to say to me, "You don't drink milk and we both know it." How this deeply strange woman knew what my dog was thinking is beyond me.

Now my old dog has a cataract situation, he's as deaf as doornail (whatever that means), and sometimes his hind leg just goes to town for no reason at all. He snores like all the hogs in hell, but the smell of waffles or pancakes can rouse my old friend from a dead sleep. I make him a special breakfast on Sundays, and he helps me with the crossword puzzle.

We've come to know each other well, Henry and I. And we depend on each other for continuity and comfort. I'll say, "Come on, Hen, it's time to go to work," and he runs up the stairs right behind me. He lies by my side, snoozing until lunch, and then he follows me downstairs where we have our midday meal and then back upstairs to work and snooze a little more. When the day comes that Henry goes off to find Buster in heaven I don't know what I'll do. Even though Buster was a sweeter dog and loved us more, Henry and I have some connection that transcends reasonable explanation, as though he's my best friend trapped in a dog's body. He understands me. Isn't that what we all want from this life? To have someone know you and love you anyway? I miss Buster every day, but there'll never be another Henry.

Dorothea Benton Frank is the *New York Times* bestselling author of *Porch Lights, Lowcountry Summer, Return to Sullivan's Island, The Land of Mango Sunsets,* and other titles. Born and raised on Sullivan's Island, she now splits her time between New Jersey and the South Carolina Lowcountry.

Impy

Marshall Chapman

I only saw my father cry once. It was the winter of 1964, the winter Impy died.

Impy was our family dog for eleven years. A black cocker spaniel with soulful brown eyes, his registered name was "Imp of Enoree." Shortly after Impy came to live with us, my family moved from Enoree to Spartanburg. At the time, we had another dog, an old Boston Terrier named Bendix. (So named because when he was a puppy, he'd snuggle up to next our Bendix washing machine and fall asleep. Mama said the heat and vibration from the washer reminded Bendix of his mother.)

Impy and Bendix and my sister Dorothy had a hard time adjusting to the move to Spartanburg. Dorothy, who was but a toddler at the time, would cry out every night, "This isn't home! I want to go home!" This went on for weeks. Impy and Bendix didn't cry out. They were too busy plotting.

After the move, my father had some men from the mill build a big dog pen in our back yard. Impy and Bendix didn't like the pen, and I wasn't too crazy about it myself. Even at five years of age, I could tell the pen was a little over the top—its chain-link sides eight feet in height, when four or five feet would have been enough. I mean, *razor wire* would have looked appropriate swirling at the top of that fence. Another

"I've often wondered why he chose our breakfast time to chew on those rats. I guess sometimes you just have to let the world know you're a dog."

thing that bothered me—and I imagine it bothered Impy and Bendix, too—was the pen's location. It wasn't really in our back yard. It was in our back *back* yard. Back behind the garage where Blue Jay Field began. To a five year old, not to mention a pair of homesick canines, the pen might as well have been in Siberia.

The first night Impy and Bendix spent in that pen proved to be their last. While my family and I slept softly in our beds, Impy and Bendix were digging a hole that became their tunnel to freedom. Come morning, they were gone like a knock on the door.

Their escape sent shock waves through our family and the community. Farmer Gray made announcements every few minutes during his morning radio broadcast on WSPA. Within an hour, someone called the station to report they had seen a black Cocker Spaniel with a Boston Terrier trotting purposefully along Highway 221 between Roebuck and Moore. A pair of homing pigeons could not have been on a more direct beam to Enoree.

Bendix died shortly thereafter. So for the next ten years, Impy was our one and only dog.

Impy was everything you'd want in a family dog. He wasn't mean like some dogs. He never bit any of us, though I imagine this had more to do with his good nature than any good behavior on our part. He always wagged his tail when he'd see you. Like he was *really glad* to see you.

From 1955 to 1959 I attended Pine Street Elementary School. I loved Pine Street, mainly because I could ride my bike to school. I can still hear the rhythmic *ching ching* of Impy's dog tags, sounding like sleigh bells, as he trotted along beside me. And when school let out in the afternoons, Impy would be there to greet me. I've often wondered what he did during the six and a half hours I was inside. But come 2:30, like clockwork, he'd be on that concrete ledge at the top of the stairs at the Boyd Street entrance, waiting. As soon as he'd see me, he'd wag his tail like crazy, his hips swinging back and forth, as he literally danced with excitement. It was like his tail was wagging his whole body. And the look in his eyes. Oh, he would just be so happy to see me!

Now Impy was a dog with dog instincts, so don't think he was some kind of saint. On more than a few mornings, while my family and I would be seated around the breakfast room table having our morning grits and eggs, one of us would spot Impy in Uncle T.B. and Aunt Lenoir's side yard, chewing on something. *Ooh, look y'all! ... Impy's chewing on a RAT! YUK! GROSS! Look Mama, Impy's chewing on a rat! Oh, God ... I'm think I'm gonna VOMIT! Impy's got a RAT! GROSS!!* And it's true. Impy loved to catch rats in our garage and in uncle T.B.'s garage next door and drag them out into the sunlight in T.B. and Lenoir's side yard, whereupon he'd commence chewing on them for all the world to see. His timing was uncanny. And I've often wondered why he chose our breakfast time to chew on those rats. I guess sometimes you just have to let the world know you're a dog.

Life with Impy coincided with the innocence of my childhood and growing up in Spartanburg. And like innocence itself, it one day came to an end.

One night in January 1964, Impy got into a bad fight with some dogs down the street. A neighbor tried to break it up by hosing them down with water, but to no avail. It was a vicious fight that went on and on. By the time it was over, Impy was pretty torn up. Despite his injuries, he managed to drag himself back to our house, where he collapsed in some bushes just outside the front door.

It was freezing cold that night, and Impy most likely would have frozen to death had somebody not heard him out there whimpering. I remember all of us running out of the house, and I remember seeing him lying there frozen in his own blood and the water from the hose. The only thing moving was his tail, which he started wagging the minute he saw us.

That fight was the beginning of the end for Impy. He was taken to the Animal Hospital out on the Old Asheville Highway, where he died a few days later.

When Mama told Daddy Impy had died, Daddy didn't say much. He just drove his car on back to the garage behind the house like he did every day when he came home from work. But instead of walking back toward the house like he always did, I saw him walk behind the garage where he disappeared. For some reason—curiosity I guess—I followed him. I snuck down to the garage, where I crouched beneath a window opening. When I peered up over it, that's when I saw him. He was sitting on a log pile with his face in his hands, crying like his heart would break. It sounded so strange.

The winter of 1964 was the winter death came to our family. First to go was my grandfather, my father's father. Everybody called him Mr. Jim. He was old enough to die, I guess, if there ever is such an age. Anyway, he died of heart failure. Then a few weeks later, Uncle Pete shot himself in the head with a shotgun somewhere in Florida. Uncle Pete was my mother's youngest brother. That night, Daddy came into the room I shared with Dorothy and sat down on the edge of our bed. I was fifteen and Dorothy was twelve.

"Your uncle Pete took his own life," he said. It was hard for us to understand why anyone would do that.

Shortly thereafter, Impy died. I guess, for Dad, that was the last straw.

Singer, songwriter, author, and now actress, Spartanburg native **Marshall Chapman** (www.tallgirl.com) has recorded twelve critically-acclaimed albums and written over 400 songs that have been recorded by everybody from Jimmy Buffett and Emmylou Harris to Joe Cocker and Olivia Newton-John. Her first book, *Goodbye, Little Rock and Roller*, was a 2004 SIBA Book Award finalist, and her second, *They Came To Nashville*, a 2011 SIBA Book Award nominee. Marshall is a contributing editor for *Garden & Gun* and *Nashville Arts Magazine* and a contributing writer to *Southern Living*, *W*, and *The Oxford American*. Currently dogless, she and husband Chris Fletcher live in Nashville.

Too Much Dog

Tommy Hays

"We can't keep her anymore," my wife said, her voice cracking as she spoke into the phone. "She's always jumping the fence, and a week ago she attacked a neighbor's dog and nearly killed it."

My wife was on the phone with an animal communicator, a woman named Wendy Jones who charged ninety dollars for a forty-five-minute phone consultation. Our twelve-year-old daughter and fifteen-year-old son sat in the living room with us, incredulous that their logical, rational, and thrifty mother was willing to pay good money to a woman who claimed she could tell us what was on our dog's mind and do so over the phone.

My wife had found the animal communicator online. She lived only twenty minutes from our house, but since she charged one hundred and fifty dollars for home visits, my wife decided to save sixty dollars with a phone consultation.

"Since communication is telepathic," Wendy Jones had written on her website, "I don't need to be in the presence of the animal."

Nor apparently did the animal need to be conscious. The whole time my wife was on the phone recounting our dog Emily's life story, Emily lay at her feet sound asleep, unaware that this exorbitantly expensive call was all that stood between her and being shipped out.

"The dog tore through the house wreaking havoc—snatching food off the kitchen counter, destroying everything in her wake, and pooping and peeing on just about every available surface."

Big, black, and furry, Emily looked part chow, part wolf. Whenever we took her on hikes, people sometimes stopped in their tracks, mistaking her for a small bear. Still, she couldn't have had a gentler nature, at least with people. She never barked, never even growled. She especially loved children and, whenever a little boy or girl came up to pet her, she lowered her head and wagged her whole body.

"This isn't the first time she's hurt another small dog," my wife told the animal communicator over the phone. She told her about Emily's first attack three years ago. Emily had escaped through the back gate when my wife had opened it to rake leaves. For years a little dog had been coming in our yard, barking to the point of frothing at the mouth whenever its elderly owner walked it past our house. The dog, about a tenth Emily's size, had gotten off its leash several times and come after Emily in our own yard. That afternoon when Emily escaped, she made a beeline for that little dog's house as if she'd been waiting for this for years. The little dog's owner, who suffered from Alzheimer's, had left his front door cracked open. Emily pushed on it, went in, and grabbed the little dog in her mouth and shook it as if to kill it. A neighbor across the street, who'd seen the whole thing, ran over and pulled her off, but not before Emily had inflicted serious injury. The vet's bill, which we paid, was over a thousand dollars. A couple of days later a uniformed animal control officer visited us, with my daughter who was nine at the time, cowering in the back bedroom, petrified that he was going to take her dog away. He left us with a fifty-dollar ticket and a stern warning to make sure Emily never got out again.

Still on the phone, my wife told the animal communicator about Emily's second attack on another small dog that had happened just a week ago and precipitated this call. Emily had leapt our fence, romped through neighbors' back yards, found a small shih tzu quietly minding its own business in its own backyard. The vet bill—sixteen hundred dollars. We couldn't afford to keep her anymore, and it was unfair to our neighbors to have a vicious dog coming on their property, attacking their dogs. As obvious as it was that we needed to find Emily another home, it wasn't an easy decision. To be honest, it was easier for me than my wife who had a real connection with Emily, and Emily, it appeared, felt the same about her, forever shadowing my wife around the house.

We'd gotten Emily as a six-month old puppy from our vet, who'd found her and her brother and her mother, malnourished and mange-eaten, wandering in a field where they'd survived scavenging for grass, roots, and small animals. Our vet noticed that Emily had a particularly sweet nature in spite of her feral upbringing and decided to put her up for adoption through her practice. Emily's brother was bad tempered and aggressive. Not feeling comfortable adopting him out, the vet brought him and his mother home to live among her dogs on her farm. Over time Emily's brother became more vicious and often attacked her other dogs. One morning the vet found him dead, her dogs apparently having had enough.

Our daughter had been six when we adopted Emily, a cute furry ball of a puppy. She'd been lobbying hard for a dog she could actually play with. Our old dog Maggie was arthritic, slow moving, and cranky. So with assurances from the vet that Emily wouldn't grow much larger, we brought her home. The first thing she did was head straight to my office and defecate. Over the course of weeks she tore up shoes, ripped up clothes, gnawed furniture, and even chewed chunks out of our staircase. And she grew to three times her size.

We'd had a fence put up in the back yard when we first moved to our house, but it hadn't taken much of a fence to keep Maggie in. Emily could jump the fence at will and would wander the neighborhood, refusing to come when we called. An electric fence we installed just inside the regular fence cut down on Emily's escapes, but every now and then if she saw a squirrel or rabbit on the other side she'd jump over anyway, yelping in mid-leap from the electrical shock.

It wasn't easy to walk her. My wife ended up at the chiropractor several times from Emily having jerked her feet out from under her in pursuit of a squirrel or a rabbit. Emily was too big and too strong for our daughter to walk. We'd found that out when she'd dragged our daughter on the sidewalk, taking big pieces of her knees. And whenever I walked Emily, I spent most of my time either jerking hard on the leash or cussing her. I'd come back from walking Emily so worked up I could hardly speak, and Emily would slink off to some far corner of the house, getting as far away from me as possible.

Emily had been a handful in those early years, but we didn't realize she could be dangerous to other dogs until that day when she'd run up the street and gone into the little dog's house. After that we'd promised the animal control officer that we'd secure Emily, and had done our best, but now, three years later, she'd gotten out again and nearly killed another little dog. She was just too much dog for us.

As we sat in the living room, listening to my wife go over all this with the animal communicator, our son finally grew bored and wandered up the street to a friend's house while our daughter, tears welling in her eyes, went upstairs to her room.

My wife stopped talking and was now nodding into the phone. I guessed the animal communicator was telling her what was on Emily's mind. I wondered if Wendy Jones had any idea what was on my mind—that she had a very sweet deal making a living sitting at home, listening to people talk to her about their animals. It said on her website that she consulted over the phone or even emailed with pet owners all over the world, that the distance or the means of communication didn't make much difference since she talked to the animal in question telepathically.

Disgusted at this woman for milking a cool ninety dollars out of our family crisis and for offering any smidgen of hope to my sad children or my grieving wife who'd grown teary-eyed over the course of the phone consultation, I went outside to cut the hedges, wondering if my wife would mind me cutting them telepathically.

But as I snipped away with our hedge clippers, hoping to reign in our overgrown abelia bush, which had over the years morphed to the size and general shape of a VW bug, I felt my anger recede and a deeper sadness slip in. What our wife hadn't told Wendy Jones was that we'd gotten Emily at least partly in response to our daughter, who was only in first grade at time, having surgery to remove what doctors believed to be a pre-melanoma that had appeared on her thigh. Our doctors now, years later, doubt that's what it was. But at the time, it shook me to my core. I obsessed on it so much I could barely look at my little girl, her face shining like pure light. She'd wanted a dog for some time, and I'd resisted. But after the surgery, everything took on a new urgency. I was the one who initiated our trip to the vet's office, and together my daughter and I looked

through their album of dogs for adoption and found Emily. Two days later my wife and our daughter brought Emily home. Those first days the dog tore through the house wreaking havoc—snatching food off the kitchen counter, destroying everything in her wake, and pooping and peeing on just about every available surface. She aggravated our old dog by relentlessly trying to play with her, and she infuriated me so often and in so many ways that once in the middle of the night when she'd woken me for the hundredth time with her whining I'd picked her up and hurled her out into the pitch black yard. In other words Emily bounded into our household like the life force she was, returning us to ourselves. Who had time for phantom worries when a dog like Emily was loose in our midst?

That night at supper my wife told us what the animal communicator had said. Wendy Jones told my wife that Emily had had no idea we were thinking of getting rid of her and she was very surprised. Emily told her she loved living with our family and wanted to stay with us. Emily told Wendy Jones that she had mistaken those small dogs for rabbits and that she hadn't known she shouldn't chase them down, and that she was sorry she'd hurt them. Emily told her she would try and do better.

My tongue was in my cheek, but it was clear that my wife had taken the animal communicator's talk with Emily dead seriously. It was also clear that our children didn't believe a word of it, but seeing a ray of hope for Emily, they resisted uttering a single cynical teenage word.

My wife said we could redouble our efforts to make sure Emily didn't jump the backyard fence. A neighbor had told her about a cattle wire that we could string along the top of the fence in the corner where she usually jumped. Our children chimed in that they would walk Emily regularly so she wouldn't get as restless. I could feel the mood at the table lightening. And that afternoon over the course of wrestling the abelia bush, I'd felt a shift within myself. That night we backed into deciding to keep her. And as if to cement that decision, the next day the woman whose shih tzu Emily had attacked brought over a check for eight hundred dollars, returning half of what we'd paid her for the vet bill.

She said she'd felt partially to blame, leaving her little dog alone in her unfenced back yard. "Besides," the woman said, "I'm thinking Emily mistook my dog for a rabbit."

Four more years have passed. My daughter, now a tall beautiful and very strong sixteen-year-old, has no trouble walking Emily, who is ten now, has grayed around the eyes and ears, who moves a little slower, and who's mellowed into an even sweeter dog. Whether it was the electric cattle wire my wife put up or the children walking Emily more often or Emily's promise to the animal communicator to try and do better, I can't say. All I know is that after that ninety-dollar phone consultation, Emily never jumped the fence again and never did she attack another dog, although just yesterday, while cutting the grass in the back yard, I came across the bloody remains of a freshly killed rabbit.

A native of Greenville, **Tommy Hays** is executive director of the Great Smokies Writing Program and lecturer in the Master of Liberal Arts Program at the University of North Carolina Asheville. He also teaches in the Master of Fine Arts Creative Writing Program at Murray State University in Kentucky. Hays is the author of four novels *The Pleasure Was Mine*, *In the Family Way*, *Sam's Crossing*, and the forthcoming *What I Came to Tell You*, which includes a small dog named Biscuit among its cast of characters.

Carolina Dog

Elise Blackwell

Looking to improve my academic life and leave lovely but landlocked Boise, Idaho, I hit the job market in 2004. The job I most wanted was at Tulane. This was not because I hold any love for that institution—I was a public school kid all the way through—but because it would return me home to southern Louisiana and land me in my favorite American city. If I'd been offered the job, I would have accepted it, bought a house, and moved to New Orleans.

I didn't get that job but was offered other good positions. I picked the University of South Carolina and in the summer of 2005 returned to the South after two decades of living in other parts of the country. I expected my San Diego-raised husband to be culture-shocked and wasn't entirely surprised that every day my daughter asked to move back to Idaho. Or back to New Jersey. Or back to California. Or to another country. But I expected to fit in. I may have lost my accent over the years, but I was still a Southerner.

What I found in South Carolina was a very different South than the one where I grew up. In southern Louisiana, *stop by for a drink* means *come on over and the sooner and longer the better*. In South Carolina, it seemed to mean *I don't necessarily hate you but please don't actually knock on my door*. Several

"Elvira, like me, was supposed to be living happily in New Orleans, but circumstances had gone awry, and she was doing the best she could in the middle of South Carolina."

neighbors asked me if we'd found *a church home* yet, emphasizing the words with eye contact that seemed calculated to look meaningful. It took me a while to understand that they wanted to know what religion we were, not so much so that they could convert us as figure us out. Some of the children I met said *yes, ma'am* so immediately and so often that it felt like a fear response. Missing, as far as I could see, were the passion for lots of music and too much food, *the joie de vivre* of Acadiana. And go cups? Forget about it. The things that were the same in my new home as my native state were the bad things: a history of violent racial politics, income inequality, mosquitoes, oppressive July heat, and cockroaches. (Calling them Palmetto bugs or the state bird makes them no less desirable in the kitchen.)

I've grown to love living here—and I've realized some of my assumptions were wrong— but my affection wasn't immediate. I cried when I stood in line for a South Carolina driver's license, wondering what had gone wrong with my life and why I had moved my family across the country, from a place they liked to a place they didn't understand. I was still in this confused state in August, when I followed the news about Hurricane Katrina, feeling at once lucky I hadn't made a new home in New Orleans and sick for being far away.

Several months later, when we were a bit more settled, my daughter made it clear that our guinea pig was insufficiently doglike to *count*. Initially she'd agreed to make do with *any pet with hair* and was quite attached to Poppy—so attached that we paid fifty dollars and moved here on a more expensive airline because it was the only one that would allow a rodent onboard. Now Esme made a valiant and ultimately persuasive four-day stand for a dog. Off we went to a shelter and came home with a yellow mutt called Elvira. About a year old, she looked to be a mix of yellow Lab, greyhound, and something smaller, with a husky's white mask. There was something a tad homely or just uncomfortable about her face, like a girl who's self-conscious because she knows she's not pretty, but she was downright beautiful at full speed. It was also clear from the start that she didn't have a mean bone in her body and that she was my dog.

She came with a standard-issue hard-luck story, but it soon grew clear that her unhappy past was of a different variety than the story the shelter had used to tug potential adopters' heartstrings. When we took her in to be spayed, the vet put her under anesthesia and shaved her belly only to find that she'd already had that particular surgery. Though a bit standoffish around strangers, she wasn't particularly fearful and—though she had few other bad habits—she thought she was entirely welcome to jump on sofas and beds. But she was terrified of water, anxious when clothes were put in boxes or suitcases, and determined never to be left alone in the backyard. (Before we put in a dog door so she could go in or out at will, she a made sure to stay between human and door, not taking any chances.) I determined that she was a Katrina rescue—maybe a dog who'd once had a good home but whose family evacuated and then couldn't find her.

For reasons that are so psychologically obvious as to be embarrassing, I was committed to this narrative. Elvira, like me, was supposed to be living happily in New Orleans, but circumstances had gone awry, and she was doing the best she could in the middle of South Carolina.

Shortly after Vi came home with us, Poppy the guinea pig fell victim to a hawk. Yet another thing I didn't understand about South Carolina was this: unlike western birds of prey, hawks here don't need open skies to hunt. A Cooper's hawk can swoop down from a tree and grab a Yorkie or a kitten—or a guinea pig frolicking in the grass—about as fast as you can blink. I chased off the hawk before Poppy sustained life-threatening injuries, but she died of shock a few hours later, just like the vet said she would. My child—who has shown non-coerced literary inclinations neither before nor since—penned forty elegies in two days, every one of them titled "Poppy." Even Vi, who'd politely taken a few bites at the hand of the sometimes ornery rodent, seemed sad.

We were now a one-pet household, but we had the sweetest pet ever, even when she did odd things, such as make leaf nests in the yard and dig snout holes in sand at certain times of the year. She was easy to train with one exception: she couldn't resist chasing squirrels and would charge even when on a leash.

One day I was walking Vi when a man maneuvering three large dogs looked at her and said, "That's a Carolina dog."

I thought of the ubiquitous *Carolina Girl* bumper stickers—another thing I didn't love about my new home—and shrugged.

"No," he said, "I'm telling you that's a Carolina dog."

Back at home I typed the words into a search engine and up popped a photograph of a pack of dogs in the rural Southeast, all of which looked somewhat like Vi and two of which looked exactly like her. *Carolina dogs*, the caption read.

I learned that Carolina dogs still live wild in parts of South Carolina and Georgia. They are a primitive breed in the sense that their DNA, instead of being well distributed like that of most modern dogs, sits at the trunk of the canine tree. (Others primitives include Korean jindos, Indian pariah dogs, Thai ridgebacks, Canaan dogs, and Australian dingos.) Carolina dogs are found in ancient Native American drawings, and archeological evidence shows they were here long before dogs arrived with Europeans.

Indeed Carolina dogs have inhabited the Southeast for thousands of years, surviving wild though rapid estrous cycles in young females, a cooperative social structure, and hunting skills. (They can whip a snake to death without getting bit.) Identified as a landrace in the 1970s by a University of Georgia ecologist named Lehr Brisbin, they have variously been called Native American Dog, Southern Aboriginal Dog, American Dingo, and Dixie Dingo. Today a few packs still live *in situ*, while many individual dogs have been captured for study or domesticated. Carolina dogs are now bred. That they have been named a "breed" is kind of funny since natural selection has served these ultimate mutts well. On the other hand, I'd hate to see these Ur-dogs disappear with their wild habitats. Smart and adaptable, even wild born Carolina dogs can make good companions for human families.

There are two competing theories about how Carolina dogs got to Carolina. Many believe they crossed the Bering Strait Land Bridge and were pressed east and south to escape resource and mate competition from wolves and coyotes. Others, noting that Carolina dogs show no evidence of having ever hybridized with coyotes, theorize that they arrived by Atlantic boat with a Clovis people who settled in Virginia 13,000 years ago.

The people were wiped out by dust storms as glaciers retreated at the end of the last ice age, but their dogs may have moved south.

However they first arrived, Carolina dogs have been in South Carolina for a very long time. Her ancestors may have traveled across a continent or an ocean, but Vi is of this place. Now I see it in the way she plays in sand and how she's completely camouflaged by the leaf dens she makes for napping. She is not the Katrina transplant I convinced myself she was but a true native. What I've learned—both from my dog and from living here across time—is that being a South Carolinian is a fine and interesting thing to be. When I renew my driver's license, I won't cry in the DMV line. And this time I might even smile for the photo.

Elise Blackwell is the author of four novels: *Hunger, The Unnatural History of Cypress Parish, Grub,* and *An Unfinished Score.* Her short prose has appeared in the *Atlantic, Witness, Seed,* and elsewhere. Originally from southern Louisiana, she directs the MFA program in creative writing at the University of South Carolina.

Life Lessons from Otto

Mindy Friddle

Dogs are grump antidotes. They delight you with their quirks. They aren't subservient so much as minions—the ultimate yes men. Dogs have their own worldview, unbesmirched by materialism. They are grounded creatures of simple pleasures—biscuits, squeak toys, long walks, and rear ends to sniff—they don't ask for much more than that.

My life is richer since living with Otto, my nine-year-old German Shepherd mix. I adopted him from the Humane Society eight years ago when he was a gangly adolescent. Sometimes I'll talk to him and he'll answer me with italicized thought bubbles. He'll share pearls of wisdom and occasional off-color jokes. *What do you get when you cross a pit bull with a poodle? A vicious gossip.*

Here are a few life lessons Otto has taught me:

There Are No Strangers, Just People You Haven't Met

Otto's gregarious nature saved him. At the shelter, he'd extend one paw between bars of his cage, desperate for human contact. His cellmate, a beagle mix, sprawled out on Otto as if he were a memory foam mattress. When we took him home, Otto brought out every stuffed animal and doll he could find and piled them in a heap on the living room floor.

"He sat in the backseat of the car with a groggy grin and swayed at each turn like a drunk in a taxicab."

Was it an offering of thanks? A lingering Darwinian impulse? Otto laughed, his dark round eyes crinkled with mischief. It was funny, whatever it was.

On walks, he is called gorgeous, beautiful, handsome, but he doesn't let it go to his head. His thick fur is pinstriped. He has the coiled tale of a husky, but his face is all German Shepherd: dark, erect ears, a long, tan nose, and two beauty marks. "Can I pet your wolf?" a kid inevitably asks when we walk by schoolyards. The other children hang back and watch, terrified by Otto's toothy grin, until the brave kid is rewarded: Otto has never met a person he hasn't licked.

Never Turn Down a Walk

When I pull out of the driveway, Otto gazes out of the window and watches me leave. From a few yards away, the light brown on his dark face resembles a mask and gives him a sneaky look. Will he recline on the white sofa? Dig out a stash of doggie porn? Toss back a few brews? It feels a little like leaving a teenage boy to his own devices, but I've learned Otto has only one obsession. When I return, he fixes me with his serious stare. *Is it time to W-A-L-K?* He knows how to spell it.

Otto has a talent for discovering when a walk is imminent. At first, he'd listen for sneakers and the creak of a sock drawer. Now, from across the house,

he can hear the whisper of nylon fibers. As I tug on spandex running pants, he rushes to his leash.

When we start on our walks, he breathes excited grunts—"happy puffs." His plumed tail is plumped, his ears at attention, and, as we head to the park, he leads with the brisk, no-nonsense stride of a hedge fund manager. Our walks are a daily immersion in nature. We stroll neighborhoods, explore parks, hike mountain trails. He isn't distracted by a to-do list or regrets from the past, not that I can tell. We've come upon water snakes sunning themselves on creek rocks, stepped over turtles, flushed out blue herons that rise with one flap like modern pterodactyls. Once, we came upon a raccoon on a tree stump, his jazz hands waving at us, before he scurried off.

If You Can't Forgive Your Enemies, You Can Always Laugh At Them

Small, yappy dogs snarl at Otto. They strain on leashes and foam with fury when Otto walks by. Yorkies and Chihuahuas seem especially outraged that Otto, whose paws are bigger than their heads, might dare to walk by their fenced yards. Otto looks them in the eyes and pees so they can watch. Take that. Why are little dogs so hostile? *Penis envy.*

Otto chases squirrels but never catches them. It's enough, apparently, to jump out of the shrubbery and nearly give a coronary to some wiry gray squirrel digging up a pecan, and then halfheartedly chase the creature up a tree. Otto just makes life a little dicier for them, an admission of his envy. *Squirrels have nuts. I don't.*

There is a neighborhood cat that likes to aggravate Otto, squirming in the dust just outside the gate. Otto begins his staccato *there's a damn cat!* bark. The cat, Jezebel, is lascivious and smug, writhing just out of reach, mewing *You can't touch this.* What's a dog to do but get frustrated? The cat is on *his* property doing her dirty, feline booty call like a pole dancer at the Landing Strip. Otto barks louder, relentlessly, and doesn't stop until finally Jezebel's ears go back and she saunters off, her tail puffed with irritation.

Brush Off Life's Indignities

Otto loves the cold, but in the summer, he stays inside. He knows where all the air conditioning floor vents are, and he survives South Carolina summers by lying on them. Only once did we make the mistake of having him shaved. Relieving him of his luxurious, thick coat would make him more comfortable. Or so the theory went. That morning, I dropped off a good-looking furry dog at the groomer's. That afternoon, I picked up a pale, skinny junkyard cur. Sans his silky pelt, all Otto had left was a Marine-buzzed white undercoat. He looked pink until we realized he was blushing. Humiliated, he stayed housebound for two weeks, avoiding the collies down the street, not to mention the neighbor's cat.

But Otto forgives and forgets. No more groomers, I promised. He agrees to be brushed outside. His thick fur perpetually sheds and comes out in fine, downy clumps that blow in the wind like dandelion seeds. The birds gather it. The chickadees especially love it, and weave Otto's fur into their moss-laden luxurious nests.

Otto also agrees to let me brush his teeth. Last year, the veterinarian pointed out Otto's smile was beginning to look beige and needed to be cleaned, not so much for cosmetic reasons—though I'm sure that factored in—but because the inflammation could spread bacteria to his bloodstream. Apparently, this is also true for people and is why your mother always told you to brush and floss. Otto had Jethro teeth, his bottom chompers were crooked as jammed piano keys. The vet suggested he come in for a teeth cleaning, a surgical procedure. My dentist includes paraffin hand waxes and lavender scented heating pads to lure in patients, but Otto's doctor offers anesthesia. The hardest part was dropping him off in the morning—no food or water allowed. I led him into the vet's office, and he turned around and pressed his nose to the door. *For the love of Dog, get me outta here.*

When I picked him up that afternoon, his leg still bandaged from the IV, he looked at me with stoner eyes. He sat in the backseat of the car with a groggy grin and swayed at each turn like a drunk in a taxicab. At home, he headed to his fallout shelter—underneath the dining room table—where he had weathered fireworks, thunderstorms, and now, teeth cleaning. He gulped the wild-caught salmon I cooked. Every night, I brush his teeth with monkey-butt flavored dog toothpaste. He lies back with a sheepish grin and submits.

Enforce the Fish Stink Rule

They say guests and fish stink after three days. Otto actually doesn't mind the fish stench so much, but he is firm about his guests not wearing out their welcome. He's made it clear he is an only dog, and plans to stay that way. He'll play the generous host with a dog and share ball throwing and biscuits, but after three days, he's tired of entertaining and makes it clear it's time for them to move along or he'll have to get medieval. Over the years, we've had a couple of stray dogs visit for a while, but we would end up finding homes for them instead of keeping them because of Otto's unwavering three-day rule. Once, a stray dropped in for a visit and meal and then, a couple of days later, trotted back up the street while Otto stared out the window, his eyes narrowed in a Clint Eastwood squint. *How dare you run freely in my fiefdom?* The dog-guest made the mistake of returning for a fourth day, and Otto's look turned Karl Rove: He schemed to corner the dog-guest alone, behind the wood shed. He jumped him. Neither was hurt, but Otto had made his point. *Time to move along, you untethered mongrel.* Do dogs plan? Do they scheme? Yes, they do.

Don't Hide Your Talent

Otto has a fine tenor voice. When he howls, his mouth forms a perfect black-lipped circle, out of which soars an aria, an ode to sirens. He sings from the diaphragm the way my high school chorus teacher said real singers do. As other dogs join in, Otto takes the lead, Pavarotti-style, holding a note until the ambulance passes. I want to put a wee cowboy hat and a bandana on him and post a video clip of him howling on You Tube. I'll send it to Anderson Cooper. He's aired sillier things—a husky saying "I love you" cannot even compete with Otto's stirring opus.

Express Joy for No Reason

Otto is afraid of Mylar balloons, mannequins with fierce stares, bullfrogs, firecrackers, thunderstorms, loud mufflers, leaf blowers, and the raucous cheering of televised Yankee games. Vacuum cleaners don't so much frighten him as unsettle him. He'll make a grab at the Dyson, trying to bite The Great Sucking Thing, before fleeing to the backyard.

But many more things bring him joy. He has disemboweled countless toys—rabbits and space aliens are his favorites—plucking out their plastic squeakers, eviscerating limbs, pulling out stuffing, so the things lie skinned and soggy, with vacant, gnawed-up eyes. He takes them outside and gives them a decent burial, which is pretty civilized of him, if you ask me. Otto once punctured a volleyball and carried the deflated thing around in his mouth with a furtive look, trying to decide on a burial site. He held it with delicate distaste, as if it were an egg sac. The ball was still hissing air when he dumped it in a shallow grave and used his long nose to shovel soil over it, as if he were following a secret canine ritual, some kind of dog dogma. Then he unearthed a moldering tennis ball and brought it to me to play. It was half decayed and did not bounce so much as thud and crumble. That didn't stop him from barking and laughing.

Every morning, Otto starts the day by running around the perimeter of the yard like a greyhound at the races. He is a rocket dog, in an ecstatic sprint, leaping over hydrangeas, jumping over the recycling bin. He makes three laps, full of frisk. What evolutionary impulse is this? To impress a mate? To ensure a cardiac workout? To appeal to Neanderthals? No reason, really. That's the point. This is what joy looks like, and it's impossible not to smile.

Mindy Friddle is the author of *The Garden Angel*, selected for Barnes and Noble's Discover Great New Writers program. Her second novel, *Secret Keepers*, won the 2009 Willie Morris Award for Southern Fiction. She lives and writes in Greenville.

Tuffy & Buckshot

Christopher Dickey

My own earliest memory of any dog was in a café, as it happens. I was three years old, barely, and we were living in Cap d'Antibes, in the south of France.

Why there? My father, James Dickey, had won his first real recognition as a poet when he received a Sewanee Fellowship in 1953, and with the money in hand—I think it could not have been more than a thousand dollars—he had quit his position as an English instructor at Rice Institute in Houston and taken me and my mother to live for as long we could afford it, and maybe longer, in Europe. My mother's mission was to keep our family functioning in the middle of the great adventure that my father wanted to make of his life, and through friends of friends she found us an old, falling-down villa below the lighthouse in Cap d'Antibes. It was the end of the summer and there were only going to be a few days left for me to play on the beach. We would stay into the cold months, far off season, when there would be little for a little boy to do. There was no television, of course, to which I had become addicted very early. There was no Miss Frances on Ding Dong School, no Howdy Doody and Clarabelle. As the days grew shorter and colder my parents would read to me. I would draw and make up stories. They made friends with a couple a few hundred yards down the street who had a son named Christian,

"Buckshot was a tough son of a bitch in his way, adventurous, and if not a hunter, certainly a wanderer."

and sometimes we played. My mother gave me little jobs like sitting on a high stool in the kitchen and watching for the man who brought the ice for the icebox. As the mistral blew, the hillside where we lived grew colder and an unshakeable chill settled in on every room in the house. The furnace in the basement had to be stoked with coal and my father would take me out to collect pine cones that I could throw into the flames. But a three-year-old needs, and demands, a lot of attention, so my mother decided I should have a dog, a little *caniche*, as my father remembered long afterward. He was as fascinated by the French word for poodle as by the animal, I think. It was a little black puppy that I named Tuffy.

I remember only a little bit about him, now. I remember, for instance, that he smelled like dust. And when I look at old family pictures, there is one of my mother holding him in her arms that makes me realize he was as much her puppy as mine. I think that probably, in that very selfish way of three-year olds, I thought he was not quite what I wanted. The dogs I loved on TV were Rin Tin Tin and Roy Rogers' "wonder dog" Bullet, both of them German Shepherds. Probably I gave Tuffy the name I did in hopes that he would be a tough, protective, magical wonder dog, too. He was not. But certainly our little *caniche* was well-mannered; *sage*, as the French say, which is a characteristic of French dogs that I have since come to believe is a result of all the time they

spend in bistros and cafés. They are, as animal trainers of old would say, well peopled.

In Tuffy's case, his café and ours was Le Glacier, which became that winter of 1954-1955 my parents' favorite place to eat. The air was thick with the smoke of black tobacco, Gauloises and Gitanes. The clientele were mostly older men, gray and pot-bellied in the rude, faded clothes of the maritime working class. There were no other Americans, no other foreigners there, at least during the winter. I doubt there was anyone as young and beautiful as my mother at any time. In one corner of the café was a pinball machine, which I wanted desperately to play, but I was too small. So my mother would order a hot chocolate for me or, sometimes, a Coca-Cola, and Tuffy would lie quietly, warmly, on the banquette beside me.

I do not know what happened to Tuffy when we left Cap d'Antibes in February of 1955. It seems to me that we gave him to my playmate Christian and his family. And, in truth, for many decades after I grew up I did not really think of him. There were so many other lives in so many other places, and so many other dogs, that Tuffy was almost forgotten. But about three weeks before my father died in 1997, we were reminiscing about those days in France and he reminded me of Tuffy and Le Glacier. "You had a little *caniche* dog," he said. I remembered the smell of dust, and then all the rest began to come back.

It's only more recently, however, that I have tried

to understand why it is that I no longer have dogs of my own. I think it must be because I have come to associate them with a sense of loss. And that is also why the dogs in the bistros of Paris have come to mean so much to me, because they have seemed to be, in their way, eternal.

A couple of years after we had lived in Cap d'Antibes, my mother and father and I moved to Atlanta, Georgia, which is where my father's family was from. He had gotten a job with the huge advertising firm McCann Erickson and done a stint as one of the Mad Men in New York City, then wrangled an assignment to the office in his home town. Our new house was on a quarter-acre lot in a new development, a small three-bedroom with a crawl-space beneath and a carport out back. Behind that was a stand of pines and behind them a tall stand of hardwoods, and behind them was a neighborhood where only black people lived. Our street was comfortably in the solid middle of the middle class of the time. "Homeowners unite!" my father wrote ironically at the beginning of one of his poems. But I know that he and my mother dreamed of going back some day, as soon as they possibly could, to Europe, even as I began to have adventures in the wilds of the back yard.

Our street was a dead end, but not neatly tied off. The road dipped down after it passed our house and the pavement just ended a few yards before a little creek through some badly drained land which the kids on Westminster Circle called "the swamp." I could find frogs and salamanders there, and had to watch out for poisonous snakes—copperheads and cotton mouths. Actually, as I think about it, the swamp was a pretty dangerous place for children. One of the boys up the street captured a snapping turtle there that was so big the Atlanta Journal ran a picture of it. And then beyond the swamp, up another gentle slope and on the edge of the freeway that is now I-75, was what we called "the desert."

I was about six, and about to have a baby brother, when my mother bought me another dog, this time a corgi puppy, which looked a little like a German Shepherd, I thought, but with short legs. My father named him Buckshot. I'm not sure why. And when the puppy was grown and a fixture in our lives, my father wrote a poem, "A Dog Sleeping on My Feet," using an experience with our corgi as a way to transport the poet into a communion with nature, with the wild, with the animal in himself. My father's poetry at that time was greatly influenced by the French surrealists, including and especially some of those less well known in the United States, like Jules Supervielle, who wrote wonderfully about the spirituality of animals. But this poem was a very simple conceit. The dog is sleeping on the poet's feet, and the poet does not move because he does not want to wake the dog, so his feet and then his legs go to sleep. But as the dog stirs in its sleep, dreaming of the hunt that is the heaven of animals, the poet himself imagines he is "on fire with the holy scent" and "Marvelous is the pursuit, / Like a dazzle of nails through the ankles."

It's okay to laugh at the idea of our corgi as White Fang. (The poem never says what kind of dog the poet had sleeping on his feet.) But you'd be wrong if you didn't think there was something of wildness in him. Buckshot was a tough son of a bitch in his way, adventurous, and if not a hunter, certainly a wanderer. Sometimes people who lived on that street behind the tall hardwoods would shoo him home to us. Sometimes he'd come back with green slime on his legs and on his belly from a hunt for salamanders in the swamp. Sometimes he'd be seen out in the desert, close to the freeway. And then, one day, he just didn't come back at all.

Maybe Buckshot was road kill and my parents never told me. Maybe he really did just go missing. Maybe he heard the call of the wild, such as it was on the fringes of suburban Atlanta. But when I realized he was gone—truly gone—I could not be consoled for a day, a night, and another day again.

Christopher Dickey is the Paris Bureau Chief for *Newsweek* magazine and The Daily Beast website. He is the author of six books, including *Summer of Deliverance: A Memoir of Father and Son* and, most recently, *Securing the City: Inside America's Best Counterterror Force—The NYPD*. He spent his late teens in Columbia.

Loving Tangerine

Dinah Johnson

I grew up with dogs, but I'm not sure that I loved them. They were just around.

Inky and Daddy were together even before my parents were married. Inky died when my father was in Vietnam, when I was six. This wasn't a traumatic event for me, but I'm sure that Daddy cried in the privacy of his bedroom when he returned. Or in the Asian jungle, tears trickling with rain on his cheeks.

When we moved to Tehran, Iran, there just happened to be a dog named Mack at the house when we moved in. I've never asked my parents what happened to him when we left. I suppose he was there to greet the next family. Then we were transferred to Heidelberg, Germany, where I had a turtle named Timothy John.

There were more places, and more places, and more puppies. But none of those dogs was *my* dog. Not even a cocker spaniel named Tangerine Jamaica, the first dog I actually bought.

I bought Tangerine for a very specific reason. To comfort my daughter, Sky, after her father died. Well, I'm not being completely honest. I think I bought Tangie for me. My little girl, only eight and a half, was clinging to me like crazy, not her usual behavior. So selfishly, the puppy was for me, to give me some breathing space in a bad situation. I figured that if she

"Oreo was that living, breathing, barking inspiration that made the final difference in Tangie's thriving. They are black and blonde. They are yin and yang."

had a puppy to pamper, I would have a little air.

I got more than a little air.

Both Sky and I were thrilled when Tangerine got a walk-on part in a local children's theatre production.

Both of us were scared silly when I thought that Tangerine had been eaten by a fox.

Both of us were angry when a lady in a hair salon made fun of Tangie's name. (Then we found out that her own children had named their new dog "Mama." Draw your own conclusions.)

And both of us were devastated when Tangie was hit by a car.

Our veterinarian declared it the worst case of neurological damage he had ever seen. Tangie had been hit on the head and was experiencing the same things a human stroke victim would go through. He set a date to put her down, but allowed us to take her home in the meantime. I told Sky that no matter what happened, I'd get her another dog. But the immediate task with Tangie was to love her up.

My daddy, the dog lover, who didn't live in our city, was there almost constantly, talking to our precious puppy. Mama was right in there too. And my brother. And my sisters. And Sky's cousins, of course. We had to squirt food and water into her mouth with a syringe. We talked to her a lot, and we held her a lot. I like to think we willed her back to life.

But actually, she willed herself back.

Though she was now blind, she decided she wanted to get up and go. She began walking around the house, hugging the walls, making a map in her mind. Her turned-under paws slowly started straightening out. She returned our love, nuzzling up under us more like a cat than a dog. She was a dog with more than one life. The vet was shocked. We were heart happy. Our little puppy wasn't going anywhere.

But I was still obligated for the second family dog. So we went out to see the folks from whom we'd gotten Tangerine. Tangie's mother had had another cocker spaniel litter, and we were able to get Tangie's little sister. Sky named her Oreo Jazzberry. (My daughter is a champion dog namer!) I will tell you, and Sky will tell you, and our whole family will tell you—Oreo was and is a guardian angel. Yes, Tangie has an unbreakable will. (And she has her sight back too.) But Oreo was that living, breathing, barking inspiration that made the final difference in Tangie's thriving. They are black and blonde. They are yin and yang.

My father died a couple of years ago. My home was the last place he spent time before that final trip to the hospital. My parents' dog, Buttercup, sat at the front door waiting for him for weeks and weeks and for more weeks and weeks. When Buttercup died, my mother, a woman who rarely cries, called me sobbing. Buttercup was her comfort and her companion, there in that enormous house, now without with her husband of over half a century. Buttercup's presence had made going back there bearable.

We wouldn't be the same family without Zane, my niece's silky terrier; Madison, my brother's Chihuahua; and of course Tangie and Oreo, our gorgeous cocker spaniels. And we all miss our precious Pekingese, Buttercup.

My veterinarian has given me a hard time because I've asked him repeatedly to help me find a new home for Tangerine and Oreo. Surprised? I've realized that, at the core, the desire to give them away is really a desire not to go through losing them, not to feel the pain my mother felt when Buttercup died, what we went through during Tangie's brush with death. I'd rather imagine them alive forever, in a chaotic home with three little boys throwing them balls and spoiling them with doggie treats.

But this will remain a fantasy. Because they are here with me, and will remain here with me, even after Sky leaves for college. If Tangie has nine lives, and shares them with Oreo, they will both be here to play with my grandchildren.

I am sure that I love them.

Dianne Johnson is a professor of English at the University of South Carolina. As "Dinah Johnson" she is the author of several picture books, including *Black Magic* and *Hair Dance.* Her biggest claim to fame is being the mother of future Broadway star, Niani "Sky" Sekai, pictured with this piece.

Zebo

Roger Pinckney

There was me and Pete and Charles, in a three-way hairpull over seven hundred acres of land, climax maritime forest and it was worth fighting over. Two miles long and eight hundred yards deep, coves and salt bays and freshwater seeps, ancient live oaks all drooling Spanish moss, shipmast pines and magnolias mothering a great snarl of wax myrtle, red bay, and saw palmetto, an understory so tight if a man tripped, he'd just hang there in midair, never even hit the ground. Ticks and chiggers. Deer, coons, canebrake rattlers, diamondback rattlers, otters, gators, eagles, and when the moon was right and the whiskey flowing, panthers, bears and swamp ground haints.

The deal had been cooking twenty years, proposed back when multinational corporations rushed to diversify billions into real estate. Halliburton Oil planned an inland lock harbor marina, homes and shops and Saudi royals visiting aboard their ocean-going yachts. Halliburton bailed but Charles still had a piece of the action so he brought in Pete to keep the deal alive. Turned out, the deal was deader than a dull-eyed mullet, and getting deader by the day, but none of us knew that, so we drew up the lines of battle.

It was a war that could have been avoided by a handshake and a handshake ended it seven years later. Meanwhile there were row upon row of dark

"Now that Pete's boys were gone, Zebo was confined to the kennel and laundry room and it was Dog-ageddon each time they dared turn him loose."

suited lawyers perched like crows upon a fencewire, depositions, recriminations, no-trespass orders liberally strewn, various threats, and sundry felonies. When it was all over there were six hundred acres gone into conservation easement, no lock harbor, and not one of Bin Laden's one hundred and twenty-odd brothers. But it was Pete's handshake and not Charles' and there followed yet another round of litigation as the former partners slugged it out. You never seen such.

Pete and I met flatfooted and breathless in the deer woods one afternoon. Now what? He had boys coming to the gun and mine weren't too far behind. All of them needed a place to hunt. And so did we. The lawyers got all the money but Pete still had the keys, a fifty-horse Japanese tractor, and an aggravating aggregate of derelict equipment, not a single piece designed to do what we needed. But why not round up a few good locals, solid level-leaded men? Everybody throw in a little, clear some land, plant wild-life food plots, indemnify the property owners against liability claims. Would I like to head up the project?

So that's how, y'all, the man banned from the property soon came to have free run of it. But it damn sure wasn't free. It took years and we never really got it right. But limping along with what little we had, we did the best we could. We broke out the snake proof boots, wore out three chainsaws. We tore the clutch out of a big tiller and then set the woods afire in what began as a prescribed burn and ended as a smoldering mess in the leaf-mold bottoms. Smoke lay heavy upon the swamps and glades for three weeks, provoking a perfect storm of community outrage. But we had beaucoup deer, all the wood-ducks we cared to miss, great flocks of doves with no sky in which to shoot them, wild turkeys so harassed by predators we never shot them at all, and quail that forever remained just a dream.

Pete's boys grew into fine young men on that ground and they took many good bucks in the process. They graduated from high school and headed off to college as my boys were taking their places. But then there was this matter of a yaller dog.

They called him Zebo, a registered three year old yellow Lab, copper complected, the color the English dogmen call "fox red." His momma was Kate, his daddy was Elvis, and he had a resume before he was even born: "very attractive, highly talented and totally lovable … perfect for competition, companionship and hunting." But still, he was a yaller dog.

Now that Pete's boys were gone, Zebo was confined to the kennel and laundry room and it was Dog-ageddon each time they dared turn him loose. Though Pete knew better than to catalog Zebo's offenses, he intimated the Missus had lost patience, most likely pillows, shoes, and furniture too. But he did mention Zebo's favorite snack, a fresh deer leg. Fore or aft, it did not matter. He could go through one in about an hour, bone, hair, hoof. "You know any young boys who might need a yaller dog?" Son #1 was close up on his eleventh birthday.

The first meeting was memorable. Fifty five pound Son #2 was sitting on the front porch step contently gnawing a stick of venison sausage when Zebo circled, nudged, rooted, expertly rolled him into a perfect fetal position and licked the sausage from between his fingers.

His first week at his new home, Zebo stole a steak off my plate, but I stole it back. He put his head through a window pane but I replaced it with cardboard. He broke the ear off my black bear rug but the wife was quick on the trigger of the glue gun. Trying to put on socks and shoes was an invitation to a tug of war and a rattling good slap was just part of the conversation. His face bore a continuous quizzical expression, like he was forever thinking, "Just give me a few more minutes and I will figure it all out." Jealous of the laptop, he would sit between my knees, leave great slobbery goobers on the spacebar while he tried to take the mouse from my hand, even when I was writing about him. When he lifted his leg and pissed all over a crate of antique wooden decoys, I figured Pete finally had his revenge.

But it was a fleeting notion. I took a good long look at this wild yellow beast. If form ever met function, it collided here in this canine trainwreck. Yes, the Labrador is a relatively new breed, only a couple hundred years old, but his bloodstock was six hundred years in the making, through the Newfoundlands and St John's water dogs, then all the way back to when men loosed their hunting falcons one final time and took up flintlock fowling pieces. A dog first to help handle fishing nets, adapted quickly to bring the game to hand. A water dog with waterproof fur, wonderfully soft waterproof ears, a rudder for a tail, deep chest, long legs, webbed feet, keen nose, loyalty and determination that can only be described as *dogged*. Hell, Zebo even came with a handle, a collar of fur a man could get all ten fingers into, perfect for dragging him over the side and back into a layout boat.

So I made myself a promise. I would wear this dog out. I would work him until he behaved. The boys would work him too and all three of them would behave. And I would bring them all to the gun together.

But alas, if a boy was as bone-headed as a Labrador retriever, he would likely see the inside of a jail house long before he ever saw the inside of a duck blind. When you work a Lab sprung from good hunting stock, you do not have to tell him what to do, only when to do it. And sometimes, when not to do it. But therein—as the Bard says—lies the rub.

Zebo was positively fanatical about retrieving, rolling his eyes, trembling like a pointer downwind of a covey at the very sight of a baton. He was an athlete and he knew it, taking great delight in artful airborne catches. If he fumbled, missed, skidded, or fell too many times, he would bury the baton in the azaleas and slink away disgusted. To preserve his self-esteem, which was not cast iron as you might presume, we presented him with a new baton, a three-bladed thing like a propeller off an old eighteen horse Johnson that skittered, leapt, and hopped like a pheasant rooster with a broken wing. The boys got him to fetch only on command, and he would do it, so long as they gave the word when the baton was still moving.

Zebo's household demeanor improved gradually and when it did not, his misbehavior was always punctuated with considerable charm. Case in point was his inordinate interest in the computer printer. Rather than shredding pages as they emerged, he would paw each into his mouth and lay it in my lap with only a minimum of perforation or slobberation. Ah, but then it came time for water retrieves.

This baton was a washed up crab pot float with an attached hank of anchor line. A good wind up and a boy with a long-armed sling could hit the water fifty yards out into the tide. But adding saltwater to the equation tripped some genetic trigger and it was Dog-ageddon all over again. Moaning, whining, leaping, trying to snatch the baton before the boys ever got a chance to fling it. No hold, no hesitation, no fear, no sense, but all redeemed by some spectacular airborne retrieves off the end of the dock.

Duck season was still some months off. As nothing is so corrosive to friendship as another man's half-trained gun dog, I'd need some help. Maybe a blank-firing baton projector? Maybe a shock collar? Maybe a waterproof shock collar, saltwater proof? Let's see, four, five hundred bucks? Six?

Thanks, Pete. Remind me to tell you about my pet alligator that needs a new home.

Novelist and essayist **Roger Pinckney** lives on Daufuskie Island, South Carolina, no bridge, no traffic lights, no traffic at all, no yoga, no yogurt, and where all the fast food has fins, fur, or feathers. He is the author of *Reefer Moon*, *The Right Side of the River*, *Little Glory* and other books.

Forgiving Ruedi
Mary Alice Monroe

Dogs are known for their unconditional love. My dogs greet me at the door with tails wagging and yelps of unrestrained delight as though they haven't seen me in years. All my dogs have been true blue. But only one dog taught me the hard won lesson about unconditional forgiveness.

Hans Ruedi was a big, block shaped, handsome Bernese mountain dog. A Swiss import, I waited months for him to be whelped, grow to ten weeks, and finally arrive via Swiss Air at Chicago's O'Hare airport. All we knew was that our dog was arriving with his brother and that the "Krüsi dog" would have the red collar.

I waited at the cargo dock for the relatively short term quarantine to be finished. I heard the yelping of pups before the attendant brought out the dog crate. We saw two brown noses against the metal grate, heard eager whimpering, and out burst two black and tan fur balls, one of whom ran directly into my arms and commenced licking my face with joy, crying, and dribbling pee. We bonded instantly and I held my breath while I looked at the collar. *Yes*—it was red! This was my Hans Ruedi and he'd chosen me!

Ruedi grew up to be as good looking as his international champion daddy and bore the natural reserve of a Berner, one that some might call aloof. He

"Gretta, the young girl with the most cause for anger, taught me that day that at the root of all forgiveness was love. "

was legendary in our neighborhood for his running greets when the doorbell rang. He'd come skidding to a crash at the door, his nails scraping my hardwood floors, to rear up and bark—a black bear of protection. Thieves broke into neighboring homes, but we could leave our garage door open and no one ever stole a thing.

Ruedi had a heart of gold and loved all of us with unconditional love. When Ruedi was six years old we moved to the Isle of Palms, South Carolina. I drove south in my station wagon with my thirteen year old son, Zack, the silver, china, shotguns, computer, and Ruedi in the far back. It was August and the drive took two hot, miserable days. I kept the air conditioning on full blast but poor Ruedi with his double mat fur coat panted for 920 miles. We finally arrived at our tiny rental house on pilings located in a cluster of similar cottages near the beach. We promptly nicknamed it "Ewok Village." While Ruedi stayed indoors in air-conditioning, Zack and I began looking at houses with a realtor, excited at the possibilities of living on an island.

My fifteen year old daughter, Gretta, arrived two days later. She'd spent the previous twenty-seven days hiking the Rockies in Colorado. She was buff but exhausted and wanted nothing more than a hot bath and sleep. The next morning Zack and I went off to look at more houses while Gretta slept in. When we returned to Ewok Village a few hours later, the little cottage was empty—no Gretta, no Ruedi. We figured

she must have taken the dog out and would return momentarily. After all, it was over one hundred degrees out there. As the minutes turned to an hour I grew frantic. At last the phone rang. It was Gretta.

"Mom, Ruedi's sick."

"What happened?"

"He had a heat stroke."

Oh no. My anxiety skyrocketed. "Where is he?"

"At the vet's."

"Which vet?" I asked, exasperated.

"I don't know," she paused. "Mom. He bit me."

My heart stopped. "Where?"

"In the face."

All I could see in my mind's eye were Ruedi's three inch canines. Now my focus was solely on my daughter.

"I'm coming. Where are you?"

"I don't know! It's a vet, over the connector. Past the Town Center. On the left."

This was in the days before cell phones. It's hard to remember how inaccessible one could be. I jumped in the car and took off for Mt. Pleasant, not knowing exactly where I was going but with an unshakable belief I'd find her. As I crossed the marshes, my hands clutched the wheel tightly and I prayed countless *Hail Mary*s. I turned onto Highway 17 and began frantically scanning the left side of the road. When I saw a fire engine, two police cars, an ambulance, and an animal control truck clustered in front of a small red wood building, my heart clenched. I knew this was the spot.

In the middle of the parking lot, in the full sun and surrounded by a metal gate, Ruedi lay sprawled on the cement as though dead. No one had offered him water or shade. My heart broke but I determinedly walked past him directly to the ambulance. On entering the confined space, Gretta looked up, her hand on a bandage over her cheek. She seemed unusually calm. I'd expected tears and hysteria. She removed the pad and I blanched. There was a two-inch, lightning bolt gash across her perfect face.

Despite my shock, I clicked into mother mode. I walked into the vet's office and asked for the phone. The two soulless assistants didn't want me to use their business line. I delivered a blistering attack on their incompetence and picked up the phone to call my husband, a physician, for advice. I knew Gretta needed stitches and we were talking about her face. While I was on the phone, the young man who had found Gretta and a collapsed Ruedi on the side of the road and had kindly driven them to the vet spoke up. He knew a plastic surgeon nearby who specialized in faces. He was the best, he assured me.

On a leap of faith, I decided to take Gretta to this unknown doctor's office. Before I left I checked on Ruedi, who was now dumped in the back of a pickup truck. I went near and tried to pet him but I couldn't reach his fur. The animal control guy told me in a flat voice, "I think he's dead."

"Ruedi!" I called.

At the sound of my voice he lifted his head, then collapsed back again. I told Ruedi I had to leave but that I'd come back. Now, I had to help my daughter.

When we returned to Ewok Village three harrowing hours later, shaken and speechless, Gretta had thirteen stitches. Later that week she began her first day at a new school. I'll never forget my brave girl stepping out from her room, her head bent so that a long swath of blonde hair covered the bandage on the left side of her face. I kept thinking over and over— *why didn't it happen to me?*

Ruedi did not die. When at last he was well enough to come home, I hesitated. He'd bitten my child. Would he bite again? I couldn't take him back. I had three vets examine Ruedi. Each of them assured me that Ruedi had been delirious and didn't know what he was doing. Likely, he didn't even remember the incident. Still I wasn't convinced.

I told Gretta that Ruedi wasn't coming back, thinking she'd be relieved. Instead she burst into tears. She cried she couldn't blame Ruedi. She'd taken him on a long walk in dangerous heat and he'd collapsed. She blamed herself for what happened and begged for him to come home. It was, I knew, her decision.

Ruedi came home weak and thin, but his dog sense picked up on my coolness. He looked mournful when I ignored him and kept him confined, no longer able to sleep with the children. Gretta may have forgiven him, but I had not.

Our lives slowly emerged from bleakness. One afternoon I came into the room to see Gretta studying on the floor, Ruedi's massive head lying in her lap as her fingers idly stroked him. It was an ordinary scene with extraordinary impact. Tears filled my eyes and I slumped against the doorframe. This was a vision of unconditional forgiveness. Gretta, the young girl with the most cause for anger, taught me that day that at the root of all forgiveness was love.

Thanks to the aid of a good Samaritan, a sympathetic and talented doctor, and the healing power of young skin, Gretta's scar is miraculously gone and she's blossomed into a woman as beautiful inside as she is out. Ruedi, a dog bred for mountains, never acclimated to sandy beaches, but he remained content with his family and air-conditioning.

Four years later, Ruedi lay his head on *my* lap for the last time. When he went to sleep and I said goodbye, my heart held no trace of resentment. It was full with love.

Today the children are grown and have moved off in pursuit of their own dreams, but we all call the Lowcountry home. I have two new dogs including a black and tan King Charles Cavalier spaniel that looks like a miniature Bernese Mountain Dog and loves to surf the waves. We have loved every dog that has joined our family. Yet, if you ask my children which, of all our dogs, was the best, they'd unanimously say—with the amnesia of unconditional forgiveness and love—"Ruedi."

New York Times best-selling author **Mary Alice Monroe** is the author of over a dozen novels, including *Beach House Memories* and *The Butterfly's Daughter*, as well as several non-fiction titles and children's books. She lives at the Isle of Palms and is involved with several environmental groups on the coast.

A Manifesto for Pet Cremation

George Singleton

Good-to-be strays thrown out in the middle of
the country by impatient and/or unready dog owners
invariably crawl on their bellies, eyes up pleading.
I've never lived with loving and judicious ex-strays
that didn't appear in my yard, then come to me as if
mimicking a Parris Island soldier-in-training forced to
crawl beneath razor wire. River showed up thusly, as
did Gypsy, Lily, and Sally. All my other ex-strays over
the years—Nick, Maggie, Stella, Marty, et al—have
been great dogs in their own ways, but they've never
fully shaken the feral out of their coats.

My dog Dooley appeared on March 1, 2000. I
went out to the front yard at dawn with my then-
nine-year-old dog River. Fog hung low. I could see
my neighbor's visiting mother-in-law a hundred yards
away, a new dog beside her. I yelled out, "Hey, Dot,
did Jim get a dog?"

With this, Dooley came running toward River and
me. River—one of those mixed breeds that looks like
coyotes—didn't growl, bark, or wag her tail. Dot yelled
back, "No. That's not our dog."

Dooley—white and liver-spotted, mostly legs, thin
as a whisper—dropped onto his belly, eyes up, with
what looked like a smile on his face. He crawled past a
Leyland cypress, a fig tree that appears to be a bonsai,
and a crabapple tree. He reached River. They touched

"I got off the bike and found—
oh, no—Marty's back leg
pushed out of his grave."

noses. I won't lie here, but—at the time Glenda and I had eight ex-stray dogs and Herb the ex-stray cat controlling us, all of which emerged from the tree farm across the road—I thought, I need to take this boy down to the Humane Society.

Dooley followed River and me inside. I put a bowl of dry food down for him and said to Glenda, "See if anyone wants a dog over at the school," et cetera.

On this particular day I had to drive down to a detention center for juvenile delinquents in Alabama in order to teach them some fiction writing, oddly. I needed to get on the road, and wouldn't return for three days. "We can't afford another dog," I said. I meant it, too.

I came back from my little trip. Dooley sat in the laundry room, chewing on the molding. "No one wants a dog," Glenda said. "He's a *great* dog. He's tried to eat through the wall and the half-door, but he's housetrained."

To this day—some eleven years later—I have no clue how hard Glenda tried to find the dog another home. And, of course, I wouldn't be spilling ink now if his presence in our life didn't make a difference.

Here's Dooley between March 2000 and Labor Day weekend 2010: Whenever I pick up car keys, he runs to the door. When there's a bird, squirrel, or rabbit somewhere outside, he's staring out the window. If I yell out "cow," "horse," or "Republican," he'll run to a window and bark. When I go off on book tours,

Glenda says, he won't eat, and barely leaves my writing room. He lived with me at Wrightsville Beach for five weeks and stared at sea birds non-stop. He's curled up below me now as I write this. River died at the age of fourteen, and since then Dooley's been the official greeter and tester-outer of two more strays that showed up. He's our largest dog, but the gentlest. He's that dog.

Now, a week before Labor Day in 2010 I had to put our dog Marty—nineteen years old—down. I buried him in the back yard next to Ann, Hershey, River, Inklet, Nutmeg, Joan, and a stray that this overzealous DNR idiot shot dead in the tree farm that we'd been trying to coax over for a month. Nineteen! One time when I wasn't paying attention, Marty—part bulldog, mostly underbite—stuck his head in my plastic cup and drank about sixteen ounces of a bourbon and Coke. He wobbled around, peed on himself, and so on, then wouldn't come near booze for the rest of his life. I buried him deep, and placed some chicken wire and a cement block on the grave.

Seven days later I ventured way in the back to ride a stationary bike that I keep out of sight so that I don't ride it too often—moderation, man, moderation—and I said aloud, "What smells? Something's dead out here."

I got off the bike and found—oh, no—Marty's back leg pushed out of his grave. It seemed as though Lily and Sally—two feisty new ex-strays—had tunneled in from the side. I shaded my eyes, for some reason, and pushed Marty back in. I dug a hole and threw that hard clay over the grave, tamped it down, put the chicken wire back down, placed some tin roofing over about a four-by-eight foot area, found some hurricane fencing to cover the tin, and then covered the area with eight cement blocks. There are smaller grave sites for world leaders than the one Marty now has.

That night, at about ten o'clock, Dooley threw up a bowl of undigested food. I said, "Damn, Dooley, what's wrong?" I cleaned up the mess

He drank a half-bowl of water and projectile vomited.

I cleaned that up and took him into Glenda's studio instead of my writing room.

He drank water, he couldn't keep it down—this went on until dawn. Even though I had done well in a college logic course, I didn't make a connection between some things. I thought that Dooley had an intestinal obstruction—one time years earlier our dog Ann ingested a number of unripe peaches that fell off the tree, skinnied up, and the veterinarian ended up giving her a simple enema that cost us $250 to get thirty peach pits out of her system.

I took Dooley outside and gave him an enema—I'll jump ahead and say that he wouldn't look me in the face for a good few days after this—but nothing came out.

I drove him into Greenville to the emergency vet clinic. This was a Sunday. Evidently it was Hit a Dog in Greenville Day, too, for Dooley and I sat there for a good three hours before a vet could see him. At this point—he didn't seem dehydrated yet, he wasn't throwing up—he seemed fine.

I took him home, he drank water, and he released it accordingly.

He could barely stand twenty-four hours later. I picked him up and got him back to the emergency clinic where a great veterinarian named Dr. B.J. Rogers—whom I'd dealt with in the past when Stella needed an emergency hysterectomy—said, "He's too dehydrated to do exploratory surgery. The X-ray shows nothing, but I know there's something in there. We can do a sonogram later," and so on.

That look on her face let me know that he might not make it. She left the room. Glenda touched my shoulder. I cried, cried, cried.

Dr. Rogers—I need to say that before she was married her name was Dr. B.J. Hogg, and that the first time we'd met I said something about how she should have been in the porn industry—came back in. I said, "Whatever it takes," but my voice came out all squeaky.

She said, "Go on home. We'll try to get him strong enough," and so on.

Back home I walked back to the dog graveyard to make sure my Marty grave hadn't been befouled by the dogs. On the way I kept finding torn pieces of towel—*the towel we'd wrapped Marty in before burying him.*

I called up Dr. Rogers and said, "You're going to find pieces of towel in his intestines. He evidently ate a towel." I didn't go into detail. I wouldn't want the veterinarian thinking that we were some kind of white trash, towel-wrapping, dog burying people in Dacusville.

She said, "Yep. We found it in the sonogram."

Dooley survived the surgery, barely. He stayed at the clinic for a couple days, but they didn't want to release him because he'd not peed. I showed up—he looked terrible—and said, "Let me just take him home." When I got him outside on a leash, he peed for ten minutes on the grass—it seemed as though he knew not to pee inside, on a concrete floor. At least that's my theory, seeing as in my mind Dooley can do no wrong.

Outside of saying to Lily and Sally, "Hey, give me that towel. If y'all eat it, you might get sick." What a martyr!

My friend Ron Rash called me up a couple weeks after this incident. He said, "What's been going on?" I started to tell him the entire story. When I got to "towel," he said, "Are you making fun of me?"

I said, "What?"

And then he told me about how his own dog had pulled a pair of Ron's boxer shorts out of the dirty clothes, ate them, and then underwent the same surgery as Dooley, by the same veterinarian. What's going on with these South Carolina dogs that live with writers? I wondered. Is there something to reincarnation? Were they critics in a previous life? I'd like to think it's the case—that Dooley once roamed this earth as a critic or editor, and that he's at my feet now, sending me high frequency advice that only I can discern. "Write about me, write about me, write about me," he's probably communicating at this very moment. "Tell everybody about my fearless exploits."

George Singleton has published two novels, one work of non-fiction, and five collections of stories, the latest of which is *Stray Decorum*. He teaches at the S.C. Governor's School for the Arts and Humanities, lives in Dacusville, and has had fiction and non-fiction published in the *Atlantic Monthly, Harper's, Playboy, Garden and Gun, Oxford American, Georgia Review*, and elsewhere. He received a Guggenheim fellowship in 2009 and the Hillsdale Award in Fiction from the Fellowship of Southern Writers in 2011.

The Odd Family

Dot Jackson

The commune, of sorts, doubtless was there before we came, but they kept strictly to themselves. It was a cruelly cold winter when we first connected with these "neighbors."

We were way out in the country, in the North Carolina foothills, on a rented fifty-acre farm. It was a heavenly place, one family's old house for over a hundred years. Old fields and pastures, fenced and cross-fenced, sloped down a cascade of blackberry-thatched terraces to a quiet, alder-bordered stream that flowed a couple of miles more into the Broad River. The farmers had died out, and the place had passed to a new owner, who had no mind to live in such a place, so he rented it to the two of us—not farmers, but newly married free spirits who loved to roam over it.

That winter was fierce. The wind howled, pipes froze, snow blanketed the fields. We did a lot of cooking, just to keep warm. Apparently the smells carried. One day I looked out the kitchen window and saw a black speck of something, struggling up the terraces, through the snow. As it got closer, it would stop and lift its nose, and sniff. It was a little bit of a raggedy black dog. Its droopy belly dragged in the snow. There had to be new puppies, somewhere.

When we went out to the pasture fence with a pan of scraps, it retreated fast as its cold little legs could

"I stopped and watched them go right to the road. On the shoulder, they all sat down, in a row. What in the world?"

go—until we were back inside, peeping out. Safe again, it scooted under the wire and ate, and ate, like that old cornbread and beans was a feast in paradise. When it backed up to go, it dragged the pan with it, until the fence wire thwarted passage, and in the pressing need to get home, it abandoned the attempt.

Next day, and every day after, whatever was left from the cook-pots went out to the back lot, and the visit was repeated once we were out of sight. Soon the pan went, too. But something else, other diners began to appear, with Little Black Dog. Half a dozen, and more, straggly creatures, mostly small—brown dogs, spotted dogs, yellow dog.

It became clear that Yellow Dog was in charge. Long, skinny legs, disreputable coat, ribs too plain for any claim of affluence, she advanced with caution on the offerings of the day, and ever watchful, ever sniffing and listening with cocked ears, policed the dining hall while all had a share.

In time they began to gather, safely down the hill, and watch for provisions to arrive. While they no longer ran at the sight of us, they let the filled tinfoil pie pans sit until we went in the house. Then, when they'd dined, like a ritual, they hoisted the pans, and under the fence they went, taking the "dinner-ware" with them.

Well, the supply was not endless, and there came the day that the assembly was waiting, down the hill, and there was nothing left to feed them in. Enough, I said to self, and went out to set things straight. "Yellow Dog!" said I, "you all have carried all the pans away and I cannot feed you till I get them back." She looked at me, surprised, and turned her thin, shabby face, with its skewed lower jaw, and protruding sideways teeth, and considered. "Ah," I said, feeling bad, "I will find something."

I went in the kitchen to decide what cookware I might sacrifice, and after a while went out with a pot of cold grits and scraps and some papers to put it on. And lo and behold, a pan had been returned. Aha! Meaningful contact had been made. At a safe distance, of course.

There was a thaw, and one day we were out on the side porch steps, where there was some sun, when we saw this odd procession coming. Yellow Dog and some kind of little feist were coming very slowly, haltingly, wobbling along, and under the fence they came, and up the yard. What was this?

As they came nearer, we saw there was something between them that they were keeping from falling. It was a little black puppy. Right up, almost within reach they came. It was the first time I had looked Yellow Dog in the eyes, which like all else about her were a little bit off-kilter, somewhat the way a Picasso dog might look. But troubled, and imploring. This puppy needed help.

"Hold on," we said to them, and I went in the kitchen and poured a pan of milk, warmed it a little on the stove, and delivered it to the bottom step, where puppy's handlers, ever wary, eased their patient forward, stood aside, and watched it drink. Only when it had fallen over, too full to stand, did the escort team step in to lick up what was left.

We wondered, should we move to pick the puppy up, to see what else to do? As if reading our minds, Yellow Dog nudged the baby up, and the trio moved decisively away, and down the pasture. She was in charge, mistress of this strange realm, and it was laid upon us that the best we could do was respect that. Yellow Dog, above all, was nobody's fool.

Some kind of peace reigned down on the branch. There was an old shed-house down there, with a caving roof, a shelter, all the same. We figured that was where they lived. Feral probably for several generations, they were more adept in the natural world than we were, by far. There was no audible ruckus down there, no barking more than an occasional yip, probably when a rabbit had been caught for a communal supper.

Only that terrible winter brought them toward us, and that peculiar connection, a meeting of the minds in which mine, I realized, was near as feral as theirs.

Dog-devilment certainly occurred out there in the country. A vicious dog pack ambushed and killed one of our aged cats. But the neighbor who saw them do it knew who they were—adored, overfed, disgusting pets with no pride of responsibility who, let loose for an occasional run, always left a trail of mayhem.

Yellow Dog's family, by contrast, was the soul of self-sufficiency and restraint.

They did grow curious about us. A cautious, touchless intimacy evolved. Once we bought a carton of ice cream and took some out on the steps as was our habit. The word got out, and pretty soon, here were a dozen eyes, watching us. *Come on!* we said. Slowly here they came. Of course Yellow Dog stepped forward first, and a taste from a spoon was startling, and thrilling. One by one, all had to taste. No demands, just fascination.

The highway ran in front of the house, a death trap for squirrels and careless domestic creatures. The wild dogs did not go there. We kept a big garden back between the house and pasture, and one evening I had put on a supper pot to simmer and was back there hoeing weeds when I noticed something very strange. Yellow Dog was coming up the yard, with the pack in file behind her.

She did not acknowledge me as she went by; she was leading with a purpose. I stopped and watched them go right to the road. On the shoulder, they all sat down, in a row. What in the world?

It was sundown when I went in the house, and there they sat, solemn as judges, watching the cars go by.

As we sat on the porch after supper, something else was strange. Country summer evenings were noisy, with chirring bugs and whippoorwills, and often the quarrels of the owls. But there was only dead silence on this night. Nothing stirred.

Until the "woman" screamed. Oh, what a wail! Somewhere, down on the branch, a woman was being killed. One of us ran to the rescue with his flashlight and his knife; we had no guns. The other called the sheriff, trying to explain: somewhere down in a blackberry hell, along a branch, a gurgling, horrid murder was in progress. All the while, the strangling victim was screeching. Until, of course, the sheriff's man arrived, and there was only silence. Stark, bugless, birdless, chilling. False alarm, the cop decided.

When the rescuer returned, sorely wounded by the briars, he said every time he got near the screamer, she moved farther down the branch. She was at least ambulatory. More odd still, her howls had an accompaniment, a little bird-like mewling song we could not fathom.

Come morning, when I saw the victim and her nocturne-singing sweetheart down in a little clearing, off the side road, they seemed in fine shape. Two cougars, not eager for their romance to be

spied upon, switched their great long tails and slipped into the willows and, like the magic that they are, were purely gone.

The birds sang with huge relief, and the katydids kicked up a joyful noise. The dogs quit the relative safety of the roadside and resumed life on the branch, unthreatened. As ever, they had taken the wiser part.

Too soon, we had to move away. A developer began tearing up creation on the hill across the branch. I wonder now, so many times, what became of Yellow Dog and her rag-tag family. They could not stay there. But they were resourceful. There were thickets and rabbits on down the stream, more provident, by her wise lights, than humankind.

She was undaunted, whatever happened. I see in my mind her earnest, whopper-jawed small face, and think of courage.

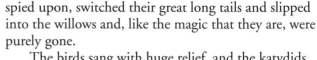

Dot Jackson, retired from newspapers, now lives in the woods at an ancient home place near Table Rock Mountain. Always most at home on the wild side, she shares this domicile (sometimes reluctantly) with all manner of creatures unspoiled by human society, from red wasps and blacksnakes to an occasional bear. She is the author of the novel *Refuge*, which received the 2006 Weatherford Award and Appalachian Book of the Year Award.

Ode to Spode

Padgett Powell

I have been writing about my dog, I discover, for twenty-two years, twice as long as he lived and he dead now eighteen years. What would compel a man who fancies himself unsentimental and sane to such a thing? The dog, moreover, was also unsentimental and sane.

In 1988, in Rome, where I was enjoying the beneficence of the Prix de Rome, in the shock of discovering that my three years of Latin in junior high school and my perusing a basic Italian book on the way to Rome did not provide me, alas, with proficient Italian, which discovery by itself suggests I did not deserve the Prix—in short, while I was hiding in Rome from Italy, suddenly Texas, where I had spent the previous ten years in a kind of civilian Vietnam tour (roofing), came into focus. Texas's pride in itself, which reduces or inflates to pride in pride itself sometimes, suddenly became a manageable nostalgia. Strange emotions are to be had if you spend a year in a country you think full of people yelling at you under the duress of comprehending nothing they are yelling. Even country music suddenly sounded good; somehow I had a tape by The Trio (Dolly Parton, Emmylou Harris, and Linda Ronstadt, I think) that I played in the high-ceilinged artists' studios in the Academy, and it sounded spectrally good, a music of the spheres with

"You were a turd, but he knew you were an okay turd, that is why he did the licking."

what may as well have been Odysseus's sirens singing it. I even envisioned for the first time getting some pointy-toe Lucheses, maybe even a hat. One morning, hungover (I was not hiding from Peroni), I composed myself and composed this:

> *Yesterday a few things happened. Every day a few do. My dog beat up another dog. He does this when he can. It's his living, more or less, though I've never let him make money doing it. He could. Beating up other dogs is his thing. He means no harm by it, expects other dogs to beat him up—no anxiety about it. If anything makes him nervous, it's that he won't get a chance to beat up or be beaten up. He's healthy. I don't think I am.*

That is a not inaccurate portrait of a boy a bit trembly from the circumstances I was in and of this dog that would come to compel me to write about him for twenty-two years. The speaker in the story is very loosely based on a small-time, would-be dogfighter I had met in Texas whom I have already in flinging him into fictitude falsely ennobled with mental capacity. But the dog is my dog, a pit bull bought five years earlier in North Carolina but essentially a Texas dog, his sire bred thirty miles (Baytown) from where I was living (Houston), his dam's main progenitors bred in San Antonio. For the cognoscenti, he was a heavy Carver dog by way of Stinson (who bred Art) and Perry and Cummings. For the skeptical who will drop the veil of Michael-Vick discreditability in front of whatever honorable utterance I might now come up with about the fighting dog, this dog was bred as well as any professional fighting dog you could buy, or steal, at that moment in the world. And that is why a sane and unsentimental man is compelled to write about him for twenty-two years even though the dog was not allowed to fight professionally. This is tantamount to saying one had a good racehorse bred in Kentucky of champion horses and one loved the horse though he was never allowed to race. The characteristics that would have made a splendid racing horse made him a splendid non-racing horse. It is a finally silly-looking argument, and I make it.

I waited another thirteen years before succumbing to the urge to memorialize the dog some more, the dog then dead seven years and my missing him only in the early fester. In 2001 I wrote this about him for the *AKC Gazette*, whose editorial diplomacy suggested that we call the dog an Am Staff if it came up (we didn't let it) and that we change, rather comically, the word *fighting* to *confrontation* and *fight* to *confront*:

A dog is the only friend you can have in life who will go with you wherever you want to go, whenever you want to go, without question and without putting on his pants. That is the quintessence of dog that secures our affection.

No questions, no pants, my dog, until he was killed at age eleven by a bobcat, was ready to go. He was capable of intimating that I was his first choice in traveling companion. No, that is inaccurate. You do not perceive in a dog the mechanism of choice, or preference, or judgment, or valuing one thing over another, and this is the second facet of the dog that wins us. He is coming with you because you are you. You? Let's go! With you, it's all good, he says, and you cannot help but love a thing that says that.

My dog would lead, get ahead by fifty feet, and select a fork in the trail and take it. If I paused at the fork, said, "Spode, this way," indicating the other fork, he would hustle back agreeably and take it. This was a complex, loveable moment: In it he said, Shucks! Alas, I presume! Goofy me! Shoulda known! You're right, boss! Better all around this way! And off he went down the path to the next fork, unabashedly presuming to pick a path there and repeat the little minuet of false humility if I again called him back. He'd do this all day, grinning.

My dog did not lie abed depressed. You don't get depression from a dog. A dog doesn't do down. This is the third magical facet in the bright furry diamond that a dog is. He's ready if you are, he's not wearing any clothes, and he's not depressed, and what on earth is better than that?

Near the end, my dog did lie abed a bit longer when he heard a noise than he would have when young. He was eleven, had no canines left, was partially paralyzed in the rear from weird coral-like ossifications on his lumbar vertebrae. So when the bobcat (if it was not an outright panther) made its first unprovoked snarl just outside his house, he let it go. When the cat made a second horror-movie noise, it was too much. He got up, creaked out there, apparently engaged big cat with no teeth to engage it with, apparently got cut pretty badly, hiked about a third of a mile down some of our path forks to a place where fish die on our property after high water, bled copiously there on his good German-steel collar, was found there a week later with the help of buzzards, and had his bones recovered there six months later, which I bleached and have boxed in a Rubbermaid Roughneck. It was not the worst day of his life. There was not a finer moment than confrontation, and there was not a finer thing to confront than an impossibly large cat—almost his size!—and if the cat prevailed, well, to him, that was another occasion for the grinning aw-shucks shrugging off of dubious judgment, so what. His collar is still in the woods, corroded by the salt in his blood to an inflexible rusty mass reminiscent of abandoned bicycle chain.

I recently was involved in the mercy killing of a bobcat struck by a car but not killed. When the game warden dispatched it with a neat, nearly invisible shot between the eyes, I took it to the taxidermist, paid $388.88, and now have it standing on two curious pieces of driftwood on my living-room floor approximately over Spode's old house under our house. The cat looks like an agreeable fellow himself, and I wish we could walk the trails together, the three of us, and delight in meaningless corrections of the way to go.

And now I am months away from sixty years old, publishing a book in which mention of this dog is a bona fide recurring element. I am in the full fester.

Spode is gone now eighteen years and I think of him almost daily. I have even made efforts to locate another dog. The breeder in North Carolina is not in dogs and reports there is not a dog in North Carolina (he means the real deal; he located a hack breeder who was in the game way back and is still breeding trash). The breeder in Texas is out of the game but has a son in the game and I was offered a dog but I wanted a puppy not a two-year-old. I lost my nerve. I may get it back. I might be, in writing this, talking myself into driving to Texas. In a moment I will tell you why. But here for now is the evolution of Spode elegy today. The speakers are two unnamed men, one of whom is claiming to have owned my dog in the lovely *Ca-n'est-pas-moi* dodge that fiction is (that is, I am talking but it ain't me):

My dog died. He never lost his enthusiasm for me. I now lament that I did not play with him more. It gave him supreme pleasure if I got down on the ground and he would turn me over to go at my face, insanely, insanely wagging happy. I should have spent all day doing this. It was a pure thing, he was unrestrainedly happy. I had the capacity to give something on earth that. There were days, weeks, I did not do this, I schlepped by leaving him alone.

You were a turd, but he knew you were an
okay turd, that is why he did the licking.

My father sold his Parker shotgun out of our
garage one Saturday morning for $20 instead
of giving it to me. I was thirteen or so. Why did
he not give it to me? I would like to have gotten
to the bottom of that, and to have talked to him
and known him at the end. I schlepped right by
all that too. But what I am saying is that I regret
more not playing with my dog. I think in this
preference I am displaying the trait or traits that
put us where we are.

Without lives, men who are not neat and
brave and Buster Brown bustamente, you mean.

We really are going to be afraid and we really
are going to also refuse to die and we will give
away the free dignity and
purchase the other expensive
dignity. I have known this
since I could not even put my
dog down. Fortunately he was
eaten a little bit by a cougar.

That was a stroke of
luck.

You are telling me.
The tail end of this was

actually written in 2009, so I have written about a dog
really for only twenty-one years. Not so bad. The full
fester of sentimentality with an asterisk on it.

Here's the deal: dogs like this are not afraid
of anything, and men afraid of things, as I am (of
everything), take great solace and cheer from being
just near that which is not afraid (and if that which
is not afraid loves you, that are afraid, it will haunt
you the rest of your fearful life). This operates very
openly at the dog pit ("At one hour," a dogfighter will
say, "I made him cur out"), and it operates at the dog
park too, or in the board room, or in the Volvo, or at
Starbucks.

I had a dog not afraid, it gave me great cheer and
blustery vicarious happiness, I am a coward now with
no blanket.

Padgett Powell has published six novels and two
collections of short stories, his latest the novel *You & Me*.
His fiction and non-fiction have appeared in *The New
Yorker*, *Harper's*, *The Paris Review*, *Best American Short
Stories*, and *Best American Sportswriting*. He has won the
Prix de Rome and a Whiting Writers Award. Having
spent some formative years in South Carolina, he has been
a writing teacher at the University of Florida since 1984.

Dog Hands

J. Drew Lanham

If you've grown up with dogs, a dog-less family seems incomplete. With our human babies out of diapers, my wife, Janice, and I agreed it was time for a canine one. It would complete the "two kids, two cars and a dog" jigsaw puzzle. We searched the listings, consulted lots of folks, and honed in on a Spartanburg kennel with an impeccable reputation. We talked to Susan Fine—were interviewed really—and met muster to adopt one of her pups. Susan originally had promised her latest litter of Labs to the state police to join the furry force of dog detectives. Instead of fetching and lolling lazily as civilian canines mostly do, the Fine dogs would wear bullet-proof vests and be issued serial numbers that would identify them as civil servants and "Property of…" It would be serious work. Luckily for us, Susan had a change of heart. At the last minute, she decided that these would be family dogs—fated for love instead of law enforcement. She made us promise that we would make him a loving member of our family.

I had other agendas working though. I wanted to do ducks. All those years watching waterfowl through binoculars—flocks of tight-turning teal, rafts of ring-necked ducks, and whistling flocks of widgeon had been fun, but I wanted more. I wanted to be closer to the wetland world that ducks seek. I wanted to watch the day break over a marsh and the day's new light glinting

"If he brought it back, cool— if he didn't, fine. Jack became a Labrador deceiver."

off frostbitten cattails and a flotilla of decoys. I wanted to learn to chuckle like a contented flock of feeding mallards or hail call and make the ducks on high hesitate and take another look—maybe for their last time.

I wanted a companion to go with me into the cold and cattails, someone who would be even more eager than I to go somewhere wet and wild. Our new dog, Jack, was to be that being. We would be there together in the first dim light of morning, watching and waiting as the whine of pinioning wings broke the dawn before the sun. We'd hunt divers—cans and bluebills—on the big water. We'd jump-shoot the hidden beaver ponds where the squealing woodies hid and would hunt the old rice fields with ducks wheeling over them thick like flies. After the hunt and a brace heavy with unlucky ducks, Jack and I would stride out of the lifting mist in slow motion with inspiring music falling from the heavens. We'd be duck-hunting gods and others would marvel at the dark-hued hunting duo—black man and black dog—masters of the marsh!

After we brought Jack home, I woke up from the *Field and Stream* fantasy. All that stuff about planning and predicting—gods laughing and un-hatched chickens—came true. The pedigree was there, replete with a regal name promising to make the partnership a can't-lose deal. I had Richard Wolter's retriever "bibles" and all the paraphernalia that guaranteed no dead duck left behind. And for a while things went according to plan. Jack ran like a wide receiver and fetched everything. The stage seemed set for more complex commands. Distance and direction would come from hand motions and whistle blasts. A wave might mean "Hey Jack, you superior sporting specimen, run exactly 173 yards that way!" Another blast and a finger wiggle would command "Now stop, look back at me, run 21.5 yards to your left, and look down. Underneath that impenetrable mat of grass, you'll find a dummy duck. Please gently pick it up and bring it to me without ruffling a fake feather." The final blast and he'd return at me warp-speed and sit like a Grecian statue to my right side, dummy duck tenderly released to my custody. "Good boy!" I'd exclaim and Jack would look at me smugly as if to say, "No problem. That all you got?" We would repeat this routine a few times in the back yard and then when duck season rolled around, we'd be ready to do the same thing in secluded swamps where real ducks, muck, and mud would replace the dummies and manicured lawn. I expected all of this to magically come together in a couple of weeks. Of course, someone would have to train me to train Jack. I quickly learned the meaning of canine attention deficit disorder. Jack would sit like the cover model for *The Retriever Journal* for a few seconds and then suddenly he was off, finding a falling leaf more interesting than anything I had to offer.

So Jack didn't get the duck-dog god memo before the kids got to him. How could any child not love a living, breathing toy? Puppies and children are made for each other. The connections between them are at least as old as the cave paintings of monstrous bison and mastodons romping across the Pleistocene plains. When the first long-legged wolf pup padded on oversized paws into a dimly-lit cave, tail wagging the rest of its scruffy body to the glee of some grinning cave kid, "Daddy" caveman probably knew that getting a good day's hunt out of the thing was questionable. Our kids spoiled Jack playing chase and tossing all sorts of non-ducky things for him to retrieve. If he brought it back, cool—if he didn't, fine. Jack became a Labrador deceiver. He reveled in it, even giving the occasional pony ride to our toddling son. With the children's dog-napping and Jack's mind tricks, I had become the trainee, fooled into taking myself a little less seriously. The waterfowling would have to wait. Jack's true purpose was not to be some bird retrieving machine, but rather to be a fully-engaged family member, just as Susan Fine had intended.

Without the pressure of performing and pedigree, Jack and I became friends. For two species supposedly separated by millions of sentient neurons and the disparities in our abilities to "know," there were more similarities between us than not. We shared beers and conversations and became *Canis sapiens* and *Homo familiaris*. We mowed the lawn together, philosophizing in the row-by-row Zen of making the grass shorter. Jack learned to expertly flip open gates with his muzzle, and if there was something outside of the chain link that he wanted, he simply reached a paw-hand out and raked it in. He used those paws like a nerd trying to solve a Rubick's Cube. I never offered to let him hold a bottle of beer but I'm sure he would've somehow managed.

And so we went on, Jack and I, friends living parallel lives but with different perspectives. As quickly as life seemed to be passing before my eyes with the kids maturing, career blossoming, and mid-life quest looming, it was speeding by Jack at seven times my rate. Although his world was largely confined to the back yard, his influence on me began to expand. Midlife presents challenges for dogs and men. I think that I might've handled it better if I'd adopted Jack's perspective earlier. Relax and let life happen—less bark, more beer.

In the summer of Jack's tenth year, my father-in-law, Thomas, was attacked by bone-eating cancer. He didn't live to see another winter's chill warm into spring. Because there were more important things to tend to, I'd neglected the yard during the stressful months of his life struggle. One day not long after Thomas's death I needed to get out and do yard therapy. I'd also lost touch with my four-footed friend. Life had become mechanical—a daily task of just getting through. Jack was happy to see me, smiling and wagging that otter tail in forgiveness. We set about straightening things up—picking up sticks and raking leaves. He fell into the Zen of it, following me around the yard on one of those late winter days when you can feel something more hopeful—like the first daffodils—trying to come on. The stress eased off with each stick retrieved. Jack seemed proud of my technique, forcing his blocky head under my hand to show his approval.

Taking a moment to catch up, I noticed his chin

was graying. "Hey man, you're getting old!" I said. Watching Thomas's life passing on I'd not noticed Jack's passing by. Suddenly I felt like I had aged seven years in that single year. In the process of bereaving I hadn't mourned personally. Like always, Jack understood that something significant had happened and he was there for me. We raked and piled the leaves. I pondered life's uncertainties in the waning light. He stuck close by, and as darkness fell we said good night and I looked forward to finishing the next day.

When I went out to gather up the leaves the next afternoon, Jack lay on his side in the sun as he often did, soaking up the warmth of the westing sun.

"Okay, Jack, time to finish up, old man!"

For the past year or so, Jack had really taken to this sunning thing. Sometimes, he dozed so heavily—snoring and twitching in deep dog REM—that I would have to roust him up. All senior citizens like the warmth that the sun brings to the aches that come with age. Jack's gait had slowed and I could tell that some days the old "giddy up" just wasn't there. He was due his time in the sun and I guessed that it was just one of those days. "Okay, Jack, time to finish up, old man!"

Jack didn't move.

He lay there in a warming patch of sun as he always did, but this time there was no greeting, no tongue-lolling, tail-wagging hello. I broke down. Jack was dead. Although I'd witnessed my father-in-law's losing battle and had only buried him a couple of weeks before, I hadn't allowed myself to cry for a man who'd treated me as a son. But now my grief for Jack and for Thomas came pouring out. Jack in his final act had opened a gate again somehow, and my tears flooded through it. In keeping our promise to Susan Fine, Jack had taught us how to let expectations fly and give in to the simpler things. He had lived mainly on his own terms and taught me much about who I was and maybe should be. Jack never saw the rising sun over a duck marsh or felt the fluff of feathers in his mouth but I believe he lived true to his life's purpose. As the sun set for the last time on my friend, I cried for all the sorrow of the past year and smiled through the sadness for all the joys Jack brought to our lives. In the seventy dog years I measured in a human decade, Jack taught me how to be more human. I miss him still.

J. Drew Lanham is a native of Edgefield and is a lifelong birder, naturalist, and hunter. His essays on how ethnicity colors perceptions of nature have appeared in a number of anthologies, and his forthcoming book, *The Home Place* (Milkweed Editions), reflects a love of nature through an African-American prism. He is currently a professor of wildlife ecology at Clemson University.

Seeing Father

Glenis Redmond

I cannot speak for my siblings—three brothers and a sister—but growing up, I always longed to have a dog. We lived all over the world as a military family: many places in the United States and parts of Europe and Africa, too. Our father believed that moving every three to four years made it impossible for us to ever own a pet, much less a dog.

Johnny Redmond, our father, was in the Air Force for twenty-one years. He loved the structure the military gave him, he enforced his own rules at home, and we had no choice but to follow his command. I loved and adored my father, but mostly feared him. Yet my nine-year-old heart wanted a dog. So much so that when our neighbors across the street were giving one away, I pleaded with my dad to lift his ban on dogs. My persistence in asking paid off: he eventually gave in and I got the puppy.

I dubbed him Sandy, because his light brown coat reminded me of the color of the sand on the Pacific beaches. We bought him dog food and I gave him a bath and found him a place to sleep. Sandy had the boundless energy of any golden retriever puppy; he brightened the household. In the end, I kept him all of five days, because later that week my dad received orders to Aviano, Italy. He broke the news that we could not relocate overseas with Sandy. Heart weighed

"He named the dog Westmoreland. I am not sure if my dad was studying Shakespeare's Henry IV at Fountain Inn Negro High School, but my poet musings imagine that's how the dog got his odd British name."

down by sorrow, I packed him up and returned him to our neighbors across the street.

That was the one and only time that I ever owned a dog. I grew up and adopted a lifestyle that didn't lend itself to owning a dog—the life of a single mom on the road six to seven months a year performing and teaching poetry.

Years after Sandy passed through my life, I visited my parents, and to my surprise there was a dog barking at me as if I were an intruder. Mom told me that the dog had wandered into the neighborhood and adopted Dad. He showed up every day, and Dad, now retired, began feeding him table scraps. Dad called the dog Scruffy and that was fitting. The dog ate what my dad ate: fried food. Over the years Scruffy remained pint-sized, though he dined on bits of pork chop, chicken, and steak, greedily and gratefully. This vagabond orphan dog brought out a tender side of my father that I had rarely witnessed growing up. Love obviously flowed between Dad and Scruffy.

Visiting Dad at this time, I began to see the jumbled jigsaw of his life—each piece was jagged, and, growing up, I didn't understand his edge. The only time I saw my dad truly soften was when he was with his first love. No, not my mother—music. When he was playing the piano by ear—jazz, blues, and gospel—he was in his own flow. As his youngest daughter, already a wordsmith, I began to understand my dad through the music he chose to play.

There was much about my father that I loved: his encyclopedic knowledge of our family's genealogy, the way he could spin a tale or deliver a joke with impeccable comedic timing. I'm not sure he knew in life how much I adored him because we had so many obstacles in our way: he was a staunch conservative, me a flaming feminist liberal. He did not understand me. He loved me in his own way, but I'm not sure he ever liked me.

When Dad retired in 1976, he vowed never to fly again. He stayed planted in his home state of South Carolina and honored that vow. Mom shared with me the secret that Dad had suffered from an intense fear of flying. I began to see my father in a greater context than I had as just his daughter. Now I saw him as a young man walking through the Jim Crow South to make a better life for his family. The irony? He left the terror of the South via the Air Force, only to live side by side with his personal fear of flying.

Although he died in 2003, I continue to learn that he was more than the hardened soldier and temperamental musician. Even after his death, my father never ceases to surprise me. For example, my mom revealed to me that Scruffy was not my dad's first dog. When he was a teenager, a dog had adopted him in a manner similar to Scruffy's. He named the dog Westmoreland. I am not sure if my dad was studying Shakespeare's *Henry IV* at Fountain Inn Negro High School, but my poet musings imagine that's how the dog got his odd British name. He set his clock to my father's; Westmoreland knew when school ended and he was always waiting for Dad at the end of the dirt road.

Looking at my dad through the lens of the dogs that claimed him allows me to have closer view of him. This vantage point allows me to adjust my sight and see him as the complex man that he was—not just a part of my physical DNA, but also part of my spiritual DNA. In the grand scheme of things, this has afforded me an expanded gaze, allowing me to see Dad in a different light and observe the whole man emerge: my view softening—nudging me toward seeing more with my heart.

Glenis Redmond is South Carolina native and lives in Piedmont. She travels nationally and internationally performing and teaching poetry workshops. She is a teaching artist for the Kennedy Center for the Performing Arts, a Cave Canem Fellow, and a NC Arts Literary Fellow.

Almost Elegy for an Ugly, Mean Mutt

Ron Rash

If I had been with my daughter that day, I doubt I'd be writing this piece, but I wasn't, so she came home with a small black dog she had immediately named "Pepper," though the animal has since been called many other names, most of which are unprintable. Pepper was and is an amalgam of not only breeds but also seemingly species: pointed bat ears, bulging salamander eyes, and a mouthful of small, sharp teeth as you would find on a piranha. As far as the dog's body structure, let's just say the Frankenstein monster had more matching body parts.

Pepper is not a stupid dog. For the first few weeks he pretended he was a good-humored, gentle creature. Once he understood that he'd been around long enough that the humans weren't going to take him back to the pound, things quickly changed. It was the canine equivalent of Linda Blair in *The Exorcist*. Pepper's first victim was one of my son's friends, who attempted to pet Pepper and was immediately rewarded with a nip on a hand. Since then the dog has bitten over a dozen people (how we haven't been sued is rather miraculous) and has shown himself pretty much able to attack from head to toe. He has bitten wrists, fingers, ankles, legs, one nose (mine, don't ask), and one butt. George

"As I stepped back to let Caroline's date in, Pepper darted out from under the living room couch and made a flying leap at the young man's crotch."

Singleton, who is as good with dogs as anyone I know, is among his victims.

Nevertheless, it is not a bite but a near miss that is most memorable. Pepper had been with us three years when my daughter Caroline was asked out on her first official date. By this time, we always quarantined Pepper whenever we knew a visitor was coming, but perhaps because it was such a landmark moment, Caroline and the rest of the family forgot. The front doorbell rang and I opened the door. As I stepped back to let Caroline's date in, Pepper darted out from under the living room couch and made a flying leap at the young man's crotch. His teeth made contact with the cloth, but hitting the zippered area, couldn't tear through cloth or skin. Ann, my wife, rushed in and grabbed Pepper and went to lock the beast in her bedroom. Caroline was still in front of the mirror so for a few moments the clearly shaken young man and I stood face to face, and alone. I taught the dog to do that to all Caroline's dates, I deadpanned, just a little reminder about needing to keep your pants on. Yes, sir, Caroline's date said, all the while nodding his head vigorously.

The young man is presently going to seminary.

Pepper is an old dog now, at least thirteen. He still attacks, but he gets to his target much more slowly. He lacks peripheral vision because of a cataract in one eye so his aim is off. Three years ago I noticed a lump on Pepper's genitals. Our veterinarian, who refuses to touch Pepper unless the dog's muzzled, found a cancerous tumor, which the pathologist's report said had metastasized. Our veterinarian operated, hoping to get "most of it" while not going deep enough to make Pepper incontinent. He'll live seven months at the most, the vet told us. *Too mean to die*, our veterinarian said a year later. I don't think he was joking. After all, why pass on when more ankles and hands yet beckon?

So as of this writing Pepper is still with us, though surely not much longer. Even he can't scare off the grim reaper forever. Now we are at the end of this brief essay. With most dogs, writers would make a final comment about how much they will miss their pets, and that is exactly what the reader expects. Yet how could someone miss this misanthropic mutt? I can't explain the how, but, damn it, I will.

Ron Rash is the author of five novels: *One Foot in Eden, Saints at the River, The World Made Straight, Serena,* and *The Cove*; four collections of poems; and four collections of stories. A recipient of the O. Henry Prize and the Frank O'Connor Award, he is a native of Clemson and holds the John Parris Chair in Appalachian Studies at Western Carolina University.

And Then There Were Three

Melinda Long

Some years back, we lost our boxer, Moses, who was thirteen years old when he died. He was the dog the kids, Bryan and Cathy, grew up with. All of us were heartbroken. Every day we watched that empty fence expecting to see a joyfully barking, drooling Moses greeting us there. It didn't seem right not to have him wagging that nub of a tail and waiting for a scratch behind the ears, but none of us could stand to go through it again. We spoke those famous last words: "No more dogs."

That lasted exactly three weeks. Before long, we gave in, made a visit to the Greenville Humane Society, and adopted Curly. Curly is a five-year-old basenji/Jack Russell mix who has height issues and likes to sleep in the closet. (Don't ask.) He can also jump four feet straight up in the air. Bryan, my youngest, was about sixteen at the time. When we brought Curly home, he jumped right into Bryan's arms and instantly became "Bryan's dog."

Curly was our first house dog. Before, we'd always had outside dogs, but Curly was an inside kind of guy. We soon discovered that inside dogs can get into serious trouble when they get bored. I returned from an author visit at a school one day to find Curly sitting beside an eight-inch hole in a new couch cushion. He gave me that twist of his head that said, *I was just gonna pull that*

"She trotted straight up to me, put her paws on my shoulders and licked my face. That pretty much sealed the deal."

one thread, then look what happened! It took me a while to convince my husband, Thom, that it was all our fault. Curly was lonely and was reaching out for attention.

Thom is an avid newspaper reader. One late-August afternoon, about a year after we adopted Curly, Thom saw a picture in the paper for the "Pet of the Week" from the Humane Society. "Melinda," he said, "look at this cute little dog! She's got great markings and she looks like she's about Curly's size. I'll bet she'd make a great companion for him. Maybe it'll keep him out of trouble." Okay, I'm paraphrasing, but you get the point. Thom, Bryan, and I went that afternoon to the Humane Society to look at the dog they had named August. We took Curly with us so he could meet her too.

What we saw when we got inside was a beautiful three-year-old dog at least twice as big as the newspaper picture had made her appear. My heart plummeted. "That won't work," we agreed. "She's just too big for us," we agreed. "No, we'll have to find a smaller dog." Yeah.

That *too big* dog turned her golden-brown eyes my way and begged to be petted. *Take me home. You know you want to.*

"Maybe we could just walk her outside and let her play with Curly," I said. "Just walk her, that's all. She's too big to keep."

My husband is possibly the most patient man in the world. "She's too big," he reminded me. "Just a walk, that's all."

"Of course," I said. I'm pretty sure Thom was already sensing defeat at that point.

She was sharing the kennel with two other dogs, and when the Humane Society associate opened the gate, August slipped past, right out into the hallway with twenty or so potential dog owners. That sweet dog never even looked at any of the other people standing around, calling her. She trotted straight up to me, put her paws on my shoulders and licked my face. That pretty much sealed the deal. I had been chosen. She knew an easy mark when she saw one.

Thom, knowing when he's been outdone, gave her to me as a birthday gift. She didn't look like an August, so we named her Lucy, short for Lucille. My son says it's short for Lucifer, but what does he know?

There is no question that Lucy is my dog. Sure, she loves everybody, but she's definitely mine. She fiercely protects me from refrigerator repairmen and delivery guys. She's a forty-five-pound Australian cattle dog mixed with pit bull, we think. Only her parents know for sure. She is white with large brown spots, lined here and there with black. Her face is mostly brown with ripples of black. Thom calls her our fudge-ripple dog. Lucy is very much the lady, especially when she sits with her front paws crossed. She also believes she's a lap-dog. Um, that could be my fault. Basically, she covers the entire chair when she sits in my lap.

As soon as Lucy and Curly set foot in the house together, they started vying for dominance. Lucy immediately corralled Curly, grabbed his back leg, flipped him over, and pinned him to the ground like a calf in a rodeo. We didn't teach her that; it came with the package. I can't say that made her the alpha dog because Curly can hold his own too, but it did make an impression.

Of course, for Thom and me, it's hard to know when to draw the line. Last spring my husband fell in love with another girl at the Humane Society. Maggie, short for Magnolia, is now the baby of the bunch. She's a Boston terrier/beagle mix that will steal your heart when she bathes your face with puppy kisses. Her tail never stops wagging. Maggie was all Thom's doing, but I was happy to bring her home. Lucy tolerates Maggie who loves to chew on Lucy's ears. She's been known to pull Maggie around the room while Maggie lies on her back and grabs hold of Lucy's collar with her teeth. Between the three of them, you'd think the circus was in town.

And of course, it just doesn't do for Lucy to see either of the other two sitting beside me in the chair while I write. If I'm sitting in my recliner, working on the laptop, Lucy has her own way of getting my attention; she lays her snout over the top of the screen. If that doesn't work, she pulls the screen down with her paw. *LOOK AT ME!* The tech from the Geek Squad at Best Buy can't figure out how the back of my laptop got so many scratches.

We are pretty much empty-nesters now. I've stopped digging out tons of cell-phone photos of Cathy and Bryan, and started displaying pictures of my dogs instead. I mean, I'm proud of both of my kids and I talk about their accomplishments all the time, but when was the last time you saw somebody look at a photo of your twenty-year-old and say, "Isn't he just precious!"

Our three dogs love without question. When I come home from a trip, whether it's been several days or just a half-hour trot to the grocery store, you'd think I'd been gone for a year. Unpacking, putting away groceries, going to the bathroom, all have to wait. I have to sit and play with my three pups until they believe I'm back for the duration.

If my husband didn't hold a tight rein on me, I know I'd adopt every dog in at the Humane Society. You would probably read in the newspaper about the crazy writer lady who lives with her seventeen dogs and knits sweaters out of the fur they shed on her couch. But the truth is that shelter dogs need a home and they have so much love for the right family. Cathy, now grown, kids me that she and Bryan have been replaced.

Not true! It's just that I'm a big believer in adopting dogs.

Melinda Long is the children's author of *How I Became a Pirate, Pirates Don't Change Diapers*, and *The Twelve Days of Christmas in South Carolina*, among others. She has been writing since the age of six when her mother, in an attempt to entertain her bored daughter, encouraged her to write a story about Yogi Bear. She's the mother of two grown kids and lives with her husband, Thom, and her three spoiled dogs in Greenville.

On the Naming of Big Dogs

Lou Dischler

Every boy should have a dog, though not every boy should get to name it. Bob is a good name for a Boxer, for instance, and Bob the Boxer was my grandfather's dog. My brothers and I would take Bob on walks down a dusty lane where he would yank us along like a husky, determined to drag us straight to the northern horizon as fast as he could. And of course we wanted a dog like Bob. A big yellow muscled-up dog like Bob.

I was six then, and my brothers were younger, so that's about the right time to teach boys about responsibility. Which was our father's rationalization when a yellow puppy appeared on our porch one night and began howling. In those days, when a dog showed up on your porch, there was nothing to do but drown it or keep it. My mother wanted to drown it, but we convinced her to let us keep it by dint of constant begging until she relented.

The cocktails we made for her helped.

We had no real idea if he would become a big yellow muscle dog, but the signs were there—the yellowness for one. Yellow dogs hardly ever became black, we reasoned. And his feet were huge for his body, which, as our father told us, meant that he would grow into them; he would become enormous. Our father also told us all the boring things parents

"I suppose this was my greatest childhood regret, that Universe didn't live up to his name."

tell their children about dogs, the long lecture about proper pet care that I don't remember today as I forgot it instantly. We all forgot it instantly as we were all concentrating on those feet, those enormously oversized feet. My youngest brother wanted to name him Bob because we expected him to become a giant like Bob the Boxer, but I pointed out that would cause confusion. My other brother suggested Jupiter, because Jupiter was the biggest planet and this dog would be the biggest dog. Naturally we got into a competition to find the name of the biggest thing of all, and that's how we finally came by his name, Universe.

Universe, the biggest yellow dog of all.

My mother hated us for this.

She hated going out in the backyard and calling for our yellow mutt, because, as she claimed with some merit, it made her sound like an idiot. Especially as Universe failed to get much bigger. If anything, his feet seemed to shrink to fit his body, and he became a neurotic little yellow dog of indeterminate breeding. It was even possible that his ancestors never had a breed. According to a boy across the street who seemed to know everything, Universe might have descended from Indian dogs, those wild camp followers that lived in the flickering shadows beyond the firelight. This was a cool idea, we thought, and it also justified keeping Universe outside at night and feeding him on an irregular basis. Being scavengers, camp dogs would eat and drink anything they could find, which is how

Universe happened to drink a bowl of Clorox I'd left on the porch to bleach cow teeth that my mother said I couldn't bring in unless I sterilized them because they probably harbored germs that would kill us all. So did cow germs kill Universe, or was it the Clorox? I can't say for sure, but he was found dead on the patio several days later, with his lips bleached white and mysterious red fluid staining his coat. This fluid was surely a clue to his death, and I invented several good if convoluted theories before my mother revealed that it was a medicated syrup that my youngest brother had poured on Universe in the mistaken belief it would bring him back to life. That syrup cost money, so my brother got whipped and learned that death was a one way trip, all in the same afternoon.

I suppose this was my greatest childhood regret, that Universe didn't live up to his name, and decades later when I went shopping for a dog at the local animal shelter to guard the mountain cabin I'd rented, I couldn't resist the dog at the end of the aisle. He was the biggest dog in the shelter, and yellow as new buckskin. A yellow muscle dog, already grown and ready to take home, which I did. A friend named him Baskerville, and that was a good name, I thought, like the Hound of the Baskervilles. In fact, he wasn't a hound but more of a Great Dane. I wasn't going to quibble, though, not after making such a massive mistake with that first dog.

I should say he wasn't a pure Great Dane, but

he definitely had a Great Dane in his background, not too many generations back. Not more than fifty, anyway. He had been quite impressive in the dark of the cage, but out in the light he showed many defects in what show people would call his conformation, and other people would call his looks. He also smelled bad, which no shampoo could cure. And worse, he moved about not with the regal air you associate with Great Danes, but with the strange stumbling gait that made you think he didn't quite realize he had four legs. Not that he used them much. Frisbees and tennis balls would fly by him unnoticed while he stood his ground.

He had but one interest, and that was watching fish.

The cabin overlooked a pond that was full of bass, and Baskerville would stand in the shallows for hours watching fish nibble at his toes. Then he would try to drink up the pond in order to get closer to the fish he loved to watch, and great masses of white foam would fall from his lips and obscure the fish. I gave him points for the irony, and I gave him even more points for his bark, which was his finest feature. It was truly a magnificent example of resonance. And so deep that you could barely hear it. So deep that woolly mammoths would have answered if there had been mammoths on that mountain in North Carolina.

There was another dog on the mountain with a bark as deep as Baskerville's, however, and he would answer from time to time. This dog was an actual Great Dane, and he was much bigger than Baskerville. His name was Goliath, which was appropriate, for he was the biggest dog I'd ever seen. My pride in Baskerville's size was shattered when, out for a walk up the mountain, we encountered this monster for the first time. Baskerville was happily chasing sheep around, as there was a herd of sheep up there too, and turned out that these were Goliath's sheep. You don't expect a Great Dane as a sheepdog, but there it was, and there was Baskerville's head, in the mouth of Goliath. I don't know how it got in there; it was so quick, like a shark attack. Goliath held Baskerville's head for a few long, terrible seconds, and then let it go.

There was no damage that I could see. Nothing physical. His ears and nose were still intact, though as ugly as ever. The only loss was his bark. As we retreated down the mountain—rather more rapidly than we'd arrived—Baskerville kept glancing back and trying his best to let Goliath have it, but nothing came out. Not for fifteen minutes, and then finally, by degrees, his voice returned. His voice returned, but not his self-confidence. The deep resonance had been replaced with the awful squeal of a rusty hinge.

God, that was sad.

Before long I began calling him Basket Case, and that was the perfect name. Once, during a party, I fashioned a dunce cap out of white paper and taped it to his head, then we watched Basket wade out in the shallows of that pond to drool over his fish. Folks drank their beers and chuckled at Basket out in the water as the setting sun turned his dunce cap into a sherbet cone, and I could see the envy in their eyes. It wasn't quite what I'd had in mind as a child, but it would do.

Lou Dischler, author of the novel *My Only Sunshine*, has lived in South Carolina for thirty years, but still writes about where he grew up. He writes about Louisiana and about dogs, and has just written a novel about a family of dogs from Louisiana that walk on two legs, which doesn't seem strange in a state where Earl Long once governed from a mental institution. He lives in Spartanburg.

The Redemption of Bo Peep

Beth Webb Hart

It was the summer of 1997, and I was in love. My boyfriend and I had been introduced six months earlier by mutual friends, and we were already talking marriage. Since I had called off an engagement to another fellow a few years before, I couldn't help but scrutinize my new man on every subject: taste in music, books, college football teams, wine, coffee, church denomination, the ability to throw a cast net and navigate a boat down a narrow and unfamiliar tidal creek. He passed with flying colors, even down to the love of domestic pets, those furry family members of which my clan of origin was never without.

My new man (Edward was his name) and I often visited my parents' home on Edisto Island because they fed us well and because they had a dock with a boat on a salt marsh creek jumping, quite often, with spottail bass just ten yards from their back door. And of course, I wanted my mom and dad's approval of the man it looked like I might marry.

Well, it took one visit with my parents for Edward to learn that the main way to their hearts was through the praise of their pets, and at the time they were in the possession of three: an old tabby cat named Angel, a black Labrador named Tuxedo and a young but scruffy apricot poodle named Bo Peep over which they had no control.

"Hmmph. So he did loathe Bo Peep. Or worse, he had a serious prejudice against one of the world's greatest breeds. But moreover, what other prejudices was he concealing?"

Bo Peep had been the pup my parents procured to fill their newly emptied nest the first Christmas after my youngest sister went off to college. They must have been weary with disciplining children and animals for nearly thirty years, so they indulged her and let her run wild. She barked incessantly, a high pitched yelp that threatened the glass in the house, and she loved to nip at toes when anyone stood up to walk anywhere. Her breath reeked, her hair was unkempt, and when she wasn't licking her crotch, she was sexually assaulting the Labrador who pretended to be asleep until he just couldn't take it anymore and batted her off his back with his enormous paw.

Nonetheless, my parents adored her. And for some reason, I kind of liked her too. I think this had more to do with the fond memories I had of the other poodles I'd grown up with than Bo Peep—canines in the possession of a good deal more social decorum, not to mention hygiene habits. And it also had to do with the recent memory of the Christmas Eve my father brought her home, cupped in a soft baby blanket in the palm of his hand, like a miniature lamb at just five weeks of age. He had put her down on our hardwood floor and she'd slid right down on her belly. We fought over her the rest of the holiday, taking turns snuggling with her in the palm of our hands as we watched movies or lounged on the ottoman in front of the hearth.

Now Edward bent over backwards to make friends with Angel and Tuxedo. He held the feline on his lap during the evening news and football games, and he'd get down on the floor and scratch the Labrador's scruff and underbelly until he yelped with pleasure. But when it came to Bo Peep, his affections were lukewarm at best. And for some reason, this bothered me.

I would notice Edward flinch when Bo Peep came out to greet us from the boat, barking her relentless and shockingly loud bark. I watched him stiffly raise his shoulders when she gnawed on our shoelaces, which reeked of fish guts, spinning herself around in circles and then following up by nipping our heels. An episode like this could go on for a good ten minutes until she wore herself out and plopped down on a tuft of Spanish moss or a small pile of raccoon or deer feces.

Of course, Edward never said a negative word to me about Bo Peep, but I could tell by the look in his eye, he was thinking as he looked down at her scruffy little body, "What is the point of your existence?"

Taking this as a red flag, some fatal flaw in Edward's character, I decided to confront him.

"Poodles are one of the smartest breeds in existence. Did you know that?"

He'd grin, a bite-your-tongue kind of grin and nod. "I've heard that."

"They're very trainable and versatile."

He'd nod and raise his eyebrows ever so slightly. Then he'd clear his throat and I would begin to stew.

Could I really marry a man who doesn't like Bo Peep?

Months passed and I put my concerns aside. Then one weekend, the weekend Edward was planning to ask my father for my hand in marriage, my best friend and her husband from the Upstate paid us a visit. They wanted to get to know Edward better so we all met at my parents' home on Edisto where there was room for everyone to gather for a few days. My friend and her hubby brought their new pet, a miniature beagle named Texas who was the about the length of a hot dog with an adorable tail that made a right angle near its tip.

The weekend went rather swimmingly, except for Bo Peep driving everyone crazy with her barking. At one point, I overheard Edward mutter to my friend's husband when he didn't realize I was behind them, "Give me one weekend with a newspaper, and I'd have that poodle all straightened out."

Hmmph. So he did loathe Bo Peep. Or worse, he had a serious prejudice against one of the world's greatest breeds. But moreover, what other prejudices was he concealing? Once the blindness of romance and that fleeting spell we call "in love" faded, would I be stuck with a man who disdained pets, children, walks on the beach, fishing expeditions, poetry, God, and all the things I loved best about life?

I was prepared to confront him on the matter as soon as the right time presented itself. Meanwhile, we all found ourselves on the dock during that perfect moment in the Lowcountry day, around five in the afternoon when the light and temperature were just right, when the tide was slack, and the water was as smooth as glass. My father brought down a cooler full of beer and some boiled peanuts for everyone, and my mother brought down a colander of boiled shrimp and a bowl of melted butter.

Just as we settled into our late afternoon bliss, Bo Peep bounded out of the house, barking like she'd never barked before, loud and frantic. Even my parents seem annoyed as they cupped their hands over their ears and told her to settle down.

Quickly, she bounded back into the house and out again, barking even louder if that is possible. Then Edward turned to look at her. She raced back in the house and then back onto the porch. Next he looked to me and said, "Do you think she's trying to tell us something?"

I cocked my head and wiped my hands on my jeans. "Maybe so."

Optimistic that he was enduring her bark and even trying to determine what could be behind it, I followed Edward up to the house to make sure all was well. As soon as we crossed over the threshold, Bo Peep led us through the den and to the guest bedroom where we found little Texas hung up by the long string of the venetian blinds, choking. Texas could anchor herself with the tip of her hind paw for a few seconds, but for the most part she was just spinning round and around, running out of breath and life.

Immediately, Edward raced to her, untangled her small body and kneeled down to hold her close as she inhaled frantically, filling up her little lungs as she trembled. Edward patted her back over and over. "It's okay," he said. "You're all right."

Then Bo Peep stepped quietly closer, looked up to Edward with her marbly little black eyes and then back to Texas before resting her unkempt head on Edward's knee.

By this time, everyone else had followed us in and as I explained what had happened, my friend took Texas from Edward's arm and made sure he was all right. (He was.)

Everyone gathered around Texas but me. I was watching Edward as he looked down at the poodle resting on his knee and tenderly began to pat her head. "Good dog, Bo Peep," he said. "Good dog."

Then Edward turned back to me and smiled—a full smile that said all I needed to know. And I exhaled deeply, assured that the man I had come to love was right for me.

The next week, we

were engaged, and at our engagement party, Bo Peep showed up, wearing a little miniature veil my mother had put on her head. (She had also put a white bow tie on Tuxedo.)

That was fourteen years ago, and while Tuxedo and Angel are long gone, I'm happy to report that my husband and I have multiplied and remain together. Bo Peep is still alive, barking as loudly and tenaciously as ever. She's a bit senile now. She growls at shadows and bumps into walls. But Edward is always delighted to see her, greeting her with a pat and enduring her awful breath as he scratches her scruff. He even picks her up when she's scared to walk up the stairs or cross a particularly slick hardwood floor. And I hold her too, along with my children, grateful that she was the one who sealed our fate and union through her unexpected redemption.

Beth Webb Hart, a South Carolina native, is the best-selling author of *Sunrise on the Battery; Love, Charleston; Grace at Low Tide; The Wedding Machine;* and *Adelaide Piper.* Her first two novels made Booklist's "Top Ten Inspirational Books of 2006" list, and her last three titles have been nominated for SIBA awards. Hart lives with her husband, composer Edward Hart, and their family in Charleston, and she blogs every Tuesday at www.southernbelleview.com.

Buddy Being Buddy

Mark Powell

In the spring of 2000 my brother James' yellow Lab, Zoe, was hit and killed by a car. He was devastated. Zoe was his constant companion, a wild embodiment of her name who never left his side, and once, in the bleakest of winters, had swam the near frozen Chattooga to perch perfectly on the bow of his kayak. So it was that summer my wife Denise and I accompanied my mom to pick out a new Lab puppy for James. It would be a surprise. The litter had just been weaned and my mom planned to take a new dog home to him that night.

Denise and I hadn't planned on falling in love with a dog ourselves, but when you are factoring cuteness on the Great Chain of Being there are Lab puppies and then, several rings down, the rest of creation. Denise found a male pup, twelve pounds of fuzz and fluff, its ears and paws seemingly full grown. That and his booty. He had the sort of wide-load bottom celebrated by the rappers popular in the early nineties when we were in high school. You held him, cuddled him, turned him this way and that, and that bottom just fell out. We took him home and my wife wrapped him in a beach towel and reclined on the couch, his warm wet nose at the hollow of her throat. I stood above them and took a photograph and it looked for all the world like she had just given birth. In hindsight I can see

"I wrote every word of four novels with Buddy snoozing at my feet, as much guardian as muse."

that as the seminal moment, because wrapped up like a little boy, treated like a little boy, he never, not even years later, not even when he weighed one-hundred-thirty pounds and barreled through the woods like—as a startled camper once described him—an albino bear, would he ever realize he was a dog. We named him Buddy. It was love at first sight.

Buddy was a mountain dog—though later he would do just fine as a city dog, all proper and refined—and almost every day Buddy and I ran along some mountain trail, Yellow Branch, the State Fish Hatchery. Our favorite was the Chattooga Trail near Licklog Falls. Four or five days a week we'd drive in listening to Van Morrison—somehow it always seemed Buddy's favorite—and run for an hour, Buddy looping wild arcs around me, sprinting ahead, sprinting behind. When the trail met the river he'd dive in and drink water so rapidly he would choke and swallow simultaneously. If we passed any sort of peak—mountain, hill—we would cut off the trail and charge to the top. I took Buddy everywhere I went because he reminded me what it meant to be fully alive. Everything he did, from running to eating—he would eat anything from a Cornish game hen to tin foil—to the marathon naps he took in front of the fire, he overdid, wild, exactly as Kerouac said we should be, for life.

Over time, he became something of a legend among our friends. The party when Buddy leaped onto the table and swallowed a three-pound cheese ball without ever moving a cracker. The time in Charleston he swam an alligator-filled swamp to flirt with a tiny white poodle—he scared her to death, but has always had a thing for poodles. The morning run in the mountains when he sniffed out a Boy Scout encampment and was greeted by eight-year-olds tossing strips of bacon he snatched from the air. I wrote every word of four novels with Buddy snoozing at my feet, as much guardian as muse. So there were feats, you'll-never-believe-this stories, but what defines Buddy is his gentleness, the burly bear little boy who still wants to climb into your lap, a little spoiled, maybe a lot spoiled, but so loyal, so tender we can never tell him no.

He seemed so much our child it was easy to lose track of the fact that while we were watching over Buddy he was watching over us. In the spring of 2007 my wife was ten weeks pregnant when Buddy suddenly took to her side. If I went near her he would stand abruptly, not exactly aggressively, but he made it clear I should come no closer. It was only two days later, when she miscarried, that we realized that for forty-eight hours, day and night, Buddy had never left her side.

The night our son was born, Buddy slept in the floor on Denise's side of the bed, something he never did. A few hours later her water broke. We flew out of bed in a flurry. Buddy yawned. I imagined he'd seen it coming for days. Three years later he suddenly began to act peculiar even for Buddy, high-strung and needy. We worried at first that he was sick, then worried that one of us was sick. A week later we learned Denise was pregnant with our daughter. It no longer seemed remarkable.

"Buddy being Buddy," our son Silas said.

Which has always been true.

Buddy's older and slower now, a little arthritic; his vision is failing; his days are quieter. We no longer run together in the woods and he climbed his last peak four years ago, a beautiful sunrise summit of Cadillac Mountain in Maine. I have a picture of us together on the peak my wife took. Buddy's tongue hangs from the side of his mouth. He appears to be laughing. He appears to be telling me not to worry, *we made it up just fine*. He still sleeps on the floor beside me at night, snoring lightly while I read. When I turn out the light I hear him exhale. I touch his wide bottom, and Buddy, knowing we are all at home, all safe, rests.

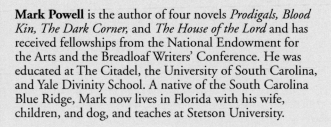

Mark Powell is the author of four novels *Prodigals, Blood Kin, The Dark Corner,* and *The House of the Lord* and has received fellowships from the National Endowment for the Arts and the Breadloaf Writers' Conference. He was educated at The Citadel, the University of South Carolina, and Yale Divinity School. A native of the South Carolina Blue Ridge, Mark now lives in Florida with his wife, children, and dog, and teaches at Stetson University.

Couch Companion

Kate Salley Palmer

I didn't know Kayla was going to be *my* dog.

My daughter, Salley, bought the black, fuzzy little ball of energy thirteen years ago—for five dollars—from a friend. Salley was coaching volleyball at Newberry College at the time, and Kayla, a Lab-chow mix, became her constant companion.

Kayla was named after one of Salley's favorite soap opera characters, and everyone in Newberry got to know her pretty quickly. Salley spent a lot of time with her and trained her well. Kayla was the only dog ever allowed in Lucy and Earl's restaurant, one of Salley's favorite Newberry hangouts. The dog accompanied Salley to another coaching position at Lander University, then to Pendleton when Salley decided to pursue a master's degree in school counseling at Clemson. There seemed to be an unbreakable bond between this young woman and her loyal, faithful dog that was lovely to see.

Then Salley met Dave.

Dave is not a dog man. He *really* doesn't like dogs.

Salley had always been pretty picky about boyfriends before, so my husband, Jim, and I thought there would be no contest—Dave would be put in a Hefty bag and set on the curb. Instead, Salley decided to marry Dave and unceremoniously sent Kayla to live with us!

"When I was able to move back upstairs, Kayla had gotten too old to leap up on our high bed, but she would sleep on the rug next to my side. "

Our previous dogs had always preferred Jim over me, so I figured Kayla would become *his* dog. But, no—probably because she preferred female owners—Kayla, in her separation trauma, latched on to me and began following me everywhere. As soon as Jim got out of bed in the morning, Kayla would jump up to take his place.

The past two or three years I have spent a lot of time on the couch because of severe back pain and a balance problem that I didn't realize was part of the swiveling vertebrae in my spine. Kayla slept on the couch next to me while I read or watched TV. In 2011 I had an operation at Emory University to fuse several vertebrae. I got bone grafts and bolts and screws and I-don't-know-what-all inserted into my back. The surgery took nine and a half hours.

But I was lucky. I had a great surgeon. When I came out of the anesthesia, it was immediately obvious to me that the surgery had worked. Though there was a lot of pain from the operation itself, the nerve pain that I had experienced in my legs for so long was gone and I could feel my left leg again!

When I got home, I slept downstairs for months. But it was okay because Kayla slept with me. I was never alone. Sometimes it was a shock to turn over in bed and find a cold wet nose, whiskers, and hot doggy breath snoring inches from my face. It was almost as if she knew something was wrong. If I hobbled to the bedroom, she'd follow. Then I'd remember I'd left something in the living room and hobble back out. She followed. Then back to the bedroom with my book or whatever. Kayla followed. When I finally got settled in bed to read or sleep, she jumped up to sleep on the bed with me.

When I was able to move back upstairs, Kayla had gotten too old to leap up on our high bed, but she would sleep on the rug next to my side.

Six months after my back surgery, everything was fine—back to normal. I was carrying the tray to my granddaughter's high chair to the sink and tripped over a watermelon that someone whose initials are "Jim Palmer" had left in the middle of the floor. My back didn't move because it is as solid as a steel girder. I landed on my elbows and jammed my right shoulder up into the joint, tearing the rotator cuff.

So it was back to the couch for me and Kayla. I could no longer use my right hand. The pain was too great. That might not bother some people, but I'm a cartoonist and need my right hand to draw or do art on my computer with a special drawing pad and stylus.

With this new injury— after just getting over major spine surgery—I decided just to lay up sorry. Not the healthiest mental reaction, but there it is. But I was still in a lot of pain and had to undergo surgery *again* to repair the rotator cuff.

During the lengthy recovery, it was—again—back to the couch for Kayla and me. I was told not to walk or swing my arms. In fact I had to really baby myself until the bones and sutures had time to do their thing.

But heal they did, thanks to another good surgeon, a lot of rehab, and the companionship of a good dog. Finally, I am fine again. I don't even need Valium for muscle spasms anymore. I save it for Kayla now, for whenever the neighbors shoot fireworks.

Kate Salley Palmer is a political cartoonist whose work is syndicated by Artizans.com. She has written and/or illustrated more than twenty books for children, plus a cartooning memoir, *Growing Up Cartoonist*, which was published by the Clemson University Digital Press. In 1998, Kate and her husband, Jim, started Warbranch Press, Inc., to publish Kate's books. She is working with her, James, an illustrator, on a new book about the Native Americans of South Carolina.

Kahlua Unleashed

Nicole Seitz

I am convinced that animals—specifically pets—can go to heaven. I began searching for answers several years ago following the death of my diabetic cat, Espresso. I searched the Bible and the Internet for anything that would validate my suspicions. *Was Spressi in Heaven?* What I found was weak at best, no conclusive statements, nothing that would set my heart and mind at ease. What finally comforted me and convinced me of my own personal truth was the evidence of the eyes.

It's all in the eyes.

I knew, without a doubt, that the cat that had licked my tears away, comforted me with his purry vibrations and "oogied" his claws in my hair to put himself to sleep, was not just an empty vessel. Looking in those eyes, I knew this creature was a Godsend, a way for me to experience some aspects of God that I simply didn't see in people. Patience. Long-suffering. Abundant joy. Unconditional love. Unending comfort. True companionship.

But then again, there's my dog.

My sweet little Chihuahua, Kahlua (Lulu), is a four-and-a-half-pound pill. She's old now, almost fourteen, and crotchety. Now that she's older, I can make excuses for her. When she barks at people as they're running by or strolling with their babies, as she nips at their heels

"She's not sweet to anyone else in the world but me. In fact, she's downright rotten, mean and embarrassing."

and legs, as she jumps up in the air on all fours, snarling and spouting doggy profanities with the triumvirate force of Cerberus, I just tell them, "She's old and mostly blind. I'm sorry. She's very protective." They look at her now with more pity than fear as they reach down to pet her cuteness and she bares her little piranha teeth and tries to bite their fingers off. I smile, scoop her up and feign, "Lulu, no, no."

Then I turn around, tuck her up under my chin, kiss her, and tell her I *wuv* her.

It's not her fault she's a rotten dog. It's mine. I take responsibility for it.

See, I'm a cat person. I grew up with cats. I understand cats. I can look in their eyes and see the mischief, almost hear the thoughts as they are similar to my own…*could I just have some peace? Who woke me up? I'm hungry already, and can somebody clean my litter box? Man, it stinks in there.*

But looking into Lulu's eyes is a different experience. She keeps her head down in her little doggy bed and only lifts her eyebrows. She's being invisible, see. She's trying to act like she's not there because she's guilty of something. She knows she's peed on the rug or pooped somewhere. It may not have just happened. It might have happened yesterday and I've not found it yet, and she's been lying there for a very long time, waiting for someone to step in it and scold her.

But I don't scold her anymore. She's old, and her bad behavior is mostly my fault. I got a teeny tiny puppy with a teeny tiny bladder when I was single and working full-time out of the house. I had never had a dog, only cats. I was utterly surprised she didn't train herself, raise herself better with a little more independence. You take a kitten, stick it in a litter box once and *voila*, you never have to worry about accidents again. And cats clean themselves. But dogs? Not so much. I raised poor little Lulu on the back porch while I was gone most of the day, and I've used enough Nature's Miracle on my rugs and carpets, I should invest in the company.

Oh, and she won't wear a leash and collar like most dogs. Thinks it's punishment. It's too heavy and makes her hang her head. She'll only wear a cat harness and refuses to be crated anymore so at night she has the whole first floor for mischief-making.

I know. I know. Shhh…

I should have gone to a trainer. I should have been more of a disciplinarian, a better dog owner. I should have done a lot of things. But I tell you what. Having this little bad dog has taught me more about unconditional love than anything else. She is God's little helper in my life to keep me grounded. When my head is getting too big from praise from readers? God gives me dog poo to clean up when I get home. The "cleaning of the poo" is a good humbling ritual.

It's why mothers begin to achieve some semblance of sainthood by the toddler years.

God loves unconditionally—and I've learned to love Lulu unconditionally. This includes all her faults. She's virtually uncontainable and Houdini-like when it comes to small crevices in fences. She's not sweet to anyone else in the world but me. In fact, she's downright rotten, mean and embarrassing. She bit the mailman one time and drew blood. Yesterday, she bit my husband. Twice. I watched her run across the street once to a huge black poodle. She jumped up to bite its neck fur and dangled there like a necklace as the dog looked around, *which way did it go, which way did it go?* One morning my tiny Chihuahua ran away from home, only to return with a stolen quesadilla in her mouth. I cannot make these things up.

Lulu can't see well, hear well anymore, and every now and again goes totally lame in her hind legs. She drags along the slippery hardwood floors. I have to carry her up and down the steps to go potty. And just when I'm terrified I will lose my little Lulu, God heals her, and she miraculously gets mad enough at a passerby to sprint across the lawn in attack.

Ah, the healing. The miracles. I see them all the time with my dog. And if that's not God speaking directly into my life, I don't know what is. I *am* my little dog. I snarl and pee on the rug—figuratively speaking. Occasionally, I bite my husband. Sometimes I hang my head and barely lift my eyes to God because I know he knows what I've done. But my heavenly father loves me anyway, picks me up, draws me close and kisses my fuzzy head. Over and over and over again, no matter what I deserve. So I do the same for my Lulu. She is, after all, a kindred spirit. And I've no doubt that when I get to heaven, all the creatures who've taught me about God and about myself will be there. I'll see my cat Espresso, along with Monday, the patient angel kitty we have now. And there, barreling toward me like a Tasmanian devil will be my dancing, yipping little Chihuahua, Kahlua, unleashed and saying, *Welcome home.*

Nicole Seitz is the author of several novels: *Beyond Molasses Creek, The Inheritance of Beauty, Saving Cicadas, A Hundred Years of Happiness, Trouble the Water,* and *The Spirit of Sweetgrass.* She is a graduate of the University of North Carolina at Chapel Hill's School of Journalism and also holds a degree in Illustration from Savannah College of Art & Design. She teaches art in the Charleston area where she lives with her husband and two children.

Sen, not Sin

Marjory Wentworth

Homes with shelves filled with volumes of Proust, Joyce, and Cervantes arouse the suspicion that their collection reflects what the inhabitants aspire to read—not what they've necessarily enjoyed. When I visit a home with pulp paperbacks on the shelves, I assume that every page has been read. Although I tend to be on the literary side, if I had to pick a genre for our dog Sen, she would best described as a Mickey Spillane—easy to read, and to the point.

Always vigilant, she barks at everyone and everything—including squirrels. She insists on digging up the yard as a precautionary measure, and unwinds with a swig straight out of the toilet, lid down, handle shaken. When I sing the Mr. Bubble jingle, she knows it's the code for a bath and proceeds to the upstairs bath and jumps in the tub once I've tested the temperature. Most mornings, my husband and I awaken to find her sandwiched between us with her head on the pillows.

When the boys were little we had a dear Old English sheep dog named Sparky. We figured his herding instincts would help keep three little boys safe. When he died we were all crushed. We knew that we wanted another dog—one that was smaller and had shorter hair—but we wanted some time to pass. We needed time to grieve.

"Recognizing Sen's bark is what saved her. It was a gut, maternal response that astonished me with its ferocity."

Sen entered our lives unexpectedly just a few months after Sparky died. A neighbor, who was driving back on Highway 17 after volunteering at The Birds of Prey Center, spotted a beagle weaving in and out of the traffic. Terrified that the dog would get hit by a car, this animal lover pulled over, scooped up the dog, and brought her home. Two weeks later, the stray dog had puppies: one that looked just like her, one that was brown and white, and one with black and white markings. The puppies were small and short haired—just what we were looking for. Our neighbor, who was a single mom suffering from lupus, was about to move. Why not take one of the puppies off her hands? The kids and I went over to check out the litter, and the little black and white one crawled over and sat in my lap. It was love at first sight. She seemed to be the mellowest one of the litter—this first impression is something we laugh about now. We brought her home and made her a little bed out of a towel tucked in to a laundry basket.

Something about the puppy reminded the boys of the little girl Sen in the Myiazaki film *Spirited Away.* Animation was their passion. They had an old stop-action camera and they spent hours making figures out of clay and shooting films. My husband is a filmmaker, and our sons have all followed in his footsteps. The vet, however, could not get the spelling of her name. Whenever she needed a vaccine or a rabies shot, a postcard reminder came in the mail addressed to *Sin* Wentworth. If she misbehaved we reminded her of her nickname.

It turns out that Sen is half black Lab, so she grew to be twice the size of a beagle. She looks like she's wearing a tuxedo with her white belly and paws, so she always appears dressed-up and rather elegant for a canine. I've learned that beagles are talkers, and Sen is no exception. They're also runners, and that lesson has been harder to learn. She started getting loose as soon as she was full grown. One foggy Friday evening she was scooped up by the dog catcher and brought to the pound up on Leeds Avenue. I was there when the doors opened on Saturday. I walked up and down the aisles peering into every cage, and I was astounded at how many dogs resembled Sen in some way or another, but she was nowhere to be found. I called the animal patrol folks, and they were absolutely certain that they had dropped her off there the previous evening. I stood in the parking lot in tears, when suddenly I heard Sen's bark. The sound was unmistakable. I walked around the back of the building, and there was Sen tied to a tree. Within seconds a very large woman from the pound came running outside, yelling at me about being out there in a "restricted area." I had already put Sen on her leash and was walking her to the car. I was so shaken up that I couldn't think of anything threatening to say, although I thought of a few choice phrases on the way home. I just wanted to get my dog home. I didn't realize that a dog's bark is as distinct as a voice. Recognizing Sen's bark is what saved her. It was a gut, maternal response that astonished me with its ferocity. I don't know what the folks at the animal shelter had planned for her, but it wasn't good. Even though Sen had chewed through just about every pair of shoes I owned, dozens of socks, a few choice bras, and a couple of pairs of underwear, this incident made me realize how much I loved this little black and white dog.

That summer we moved to Mt. Pleasant. On the Fourth of July I threw my back out and had a couple of herniated disks. I was in excruciating pain. I was in bed for weeks, and Sen never left my side. She was an enormous source of comfort as animals so often are in times of illness or injury. One night, my sons brought the video of *Spirited Away*. By now, the film had won an Academy Award for Best Animated Feature. My sons gathered around me and Sen slept at the foot of the bed. I was completely charmed by the movie, which tells the story of a little girl who moves to a new neighborhood with her family.

Her parents are turned into pigs by a witch and they become trapped in a parallel universe inhabited by spirits and monsters. Ten-year-old Sen bravely enters this world, where she has to fight all sorts of demons and ultimately frees herself and her parents. I moved six or seven times by the time I was ten years old. Each neighborhood was frightening, foreign, and completely overwhelming, so I connected to the film in a surprisingly personal way. Our dog's name took on an entirely new meaning.

Sen no longer eats my socks and shoes, and she has mellowed a bit with age. I know if anyone in our family suddenly enters a parallel universe inhabited by demons, Sen will run there as fast as she can, fight the evil spirits and free us from the evil forces. We are the center of her universe, and there's no place I'd rather be.

Marjory Wentworth's books of poetry include *Noticing Eden, Despite Gravity,* and *The Endless Repetition of an Ordinary Miracle.* She is the co-writer with Juan Mendez of *Taking a Stand, The Evolution of Human Rights* and the author of the children's story *Shackles.* She lives in Mount Pleasant and is the Poet Laureate of South Carolina.

A Name You Can Yell

Janna McMahan

My father has a restless heart. He's a man of action, that certain breed who begins to fidget and cast longing glances out windows when he's inside too long. Early in life, I learned that time spent with my dad was usually on his terms, in his world of wrenches and screwdrivers, basketballs and water skis, fishing poles and shotguns.

My father, who everyone calls Bobby, was never one for a hammock or easy chair. If you were with him you were working hard or playing hard. He never treated me with caution because I was a girl. I water skied, played softball, and shot hoops and skeet. My little brother and I enjoyed being around an adult who was physical and tireless. He was happy for us to tag along, as long as we could keep up.

Dad also liked dogs that matched his energy and shared his passions, which made birddogs a natural fit. To my father, dogs were not pets but companions in the field. He spent summers training a pup for fall hunting season. He selected his little athletes carefully for temperament, confidence, attention span, pointing instinct, and ability to carry objects. Dad wasn't concerned with bloodlines and papers. Pedigrees didn't matter as much as reputation. In Dad's world, dogs were traded through word-of-mouth and a handshake (even though birddog traders were notorious liars).

"He believed in pragmatic training that made sturdy, compliant animals, dogs that would take discipline and not hold it against him."

When it came time to train pups, Dad used a fishing pole to trail a bird wing or a piece of cloth through our yard. My brother and I looked on as the more talented puppies zeroed in, froze on wobbly legs, inched forward and froze again. Dad was patient and encouraging. He had a way with dogs, and like his children, these pups craved his approval and wanted to be included in his adventures.

Shortly after we returned to school each fall our father always disappeared, sometimes for weeks at a time. He lived a mystery life in backwoods motel rooms filled with camo-clad hunting buddies, gleaming guns, and malodorous dogs. He visited exotic sounding places like Nebraska and Kansas and Georgia, grain states plentiful with quail and pheasant. I envisioned him climbing fences and walking miles, his heavy shotgun balanced on one shoulder, autumn falling around him, crumbling under his steps.

Once my father asked if I'd like to name one of his new pups. As any young girl would, I picked something cute that fit a curly-eared puppy, perhaps Baby or Lily. My father was quick to crush my creativity with practicality.

"Janna," he said. "That won't work. You've got to name a dog a name you can yell. I have to be able to call them back. Something strong like Sam or Bud."

I often thought of that concept later and would stand outside and belt out a name to see what it sounded like on the wind. Some names did indeed carry with power while others melted on my tongue.

I yelled my own name. I yelled my brother's. Our names traveled. It was true that we always heard our parents' calls even from deep woods. Had we also been given names you could yell?

One spring day my father came home with a pitiful excuse for a puppy. Usually the pups he selected were bursting with energy, but this one was in a sorry state of health, skinny and sad and eaten raw with mange, a castoff from an overabundant litter.

My mother ran a tub of warm water and Dad added mange control. Mom cupped the puppy's head, holding it over the side of the tub away from the biting gaseous odor while my father bathed him. Barely eight weeks old, the pup shivered at the medicine's sting, but he never nipped or struggled. When he was lifted out, tiny mites peppered the concrete basement floor around him.

It took three dips before the pup recovered. During the last dip session my dad asked, "So, what should we call him?"

The poor creature scratched and trembled and looked at us with doleful eyes.

"How about Itch?" my mother said.

"Itch?" Dad said, trying it on for size. "Whatta ya say, boy? You an Itch? You look like an Itch to me."

Dad gave his razor-sharp whistle and the pup's ears perked up.

"Itch," he said, a decisive monosyllabic word. "Come here, boy." The pup, all gangly legs and jumbo feet, bumbled over to him. The name stuck.

Itch was half setter and half pointer, the kind of dog called a dropper. When his fur came back he had the close-cropped coat of a pointer, but the lemon and white coloration of a setter. In birddog speak, lemon is a light brown, unusual for pointers that tend to run to the rich dark brown hunters called liver.

Because of his health issues, Itch got to live in a pen close to our house rather than out of sight in the bottoms on the dog runs. He was a sweet-natured animal and since we weren't allowed house pets, my brother and I set about making Itch into our dog. We fed him table scraps and tried our best to turn him into a lapdog. But our father felt hardscrabble living conditions were necessary to make a dog hardy enough to handle long hunts in raw weather. He believed in pragmatic training that made sturdy, compliant animals, dogs that would take discipline and not hold it against him.

His methods worked well because when it came time to hunt, my dad's dogs were ready to go. He'd say, "Let's go get some birds," and the dogs would spring high into the air, all sinew and eagerness. They would sprint to the end of their run and race back to their master. He'd unhook their collars and wave toward the house. "Go get in your box!" They'd tear up the bank and bound into the back of the waiting truck. Their nails scratched frantically on the hollow truck bed as they jockeyed to stuff themselves into the gnawed opening of the wooden dog box.

My father said Itch had a lot of hunt in him. As a yearling, Itch showed great discipline, hunted where Dad wanted him to, always staying in site and responding to hand signals. When Dad's dogs worked a field, noses to the ground, they often covered twenty miles or more in a day. He kept close watch on his dogs, never letting them hunt too wide, marking their progress by the ripples atop fields of grain. When one dog got a good whiff of bird and went rigid, the rest of the pack honored the point and froze in place, too.

Dad would ease up behind his dogs, flush the covey, and pick off the quail on the wing. Afterward he'd holler, "Dead, dead, dead", the cue to retrieve. Like offerings to a god, his dogs dropped birds at his feet and sprinted back into the field for more. Dad's favorite part of a hunt was watching his dogs work.

My father kept an old station wagon thick with hay in the back. After a long hunt he'd let down the gate and his four-legged creatures would pile in. Only Itch refused to get in with the other dogs. He'd wait until Dad invited him into the front seat where he would lie with his head on my father's leg and snooze all the way home. Itch was never the Superpup that hunters seek, but Dad still speaks of him with affection. Somehow, Itch became just a little more than a birddog to my father.

After six heart bypasses in his late fifties, my father gave away his last birddog. He could no longer tote a heavy gun through miles of brush, climb fences and keep up. Still a crack shot, he has turned to trap shooting as a hobby, and now in his seventies he frequently wins his age category in national events

While my mother displays photos of her children around the house, my father has photos from trips with his hunting buddies, caps pushed back on their heads, guns across their knees. They mug for the camera, a cache of dead birds arrayed at their feet. Often there are dogs in these pictures smiling their lopsided smiles, tired and proud of the day's take.

My father had more than thirty birddogs in his hunting career. He traded and bought and sold dogs, always looking for the ones with talent and a great desire to hunt. When these dogs grew old he found new owners who promised to continue to hunt them. Dad felt it inhumane to tie down a hunting dog even though they were good for only a few hours in the field.

In a similar way, I'm sometimes concerned for my father's restless, now wounded heart. For a man of action his days must seem terribly tame, but he will tell you that he has hunted wide in life. Just ask. He has plenty of stories and photographs to prove it.

Janna McMahan, a native Kentuckian and resident of Columbia, began writing stories in fifth grade. She has since won a number of literary awards for her short fiction and is the national best-selling author of the novels *Calling Home, The Ocean Inside,* and *Decorations.* Find out more about her books, including new novel, *Anonymity,* at JannaMcMahan.com.

HUB CITY PRESS

Hub City Press is an independent press in Spartanburg, South Carolina, that publishes well-crafted, high-quality works by new and established authors, with an emphasis on the Southern experience. We are committed to high-caliber novels, short stories, poetry, plays, memoir, and works emphasizing regional culture and history. We are particularly interested in books with a strong sense of place.

Hub City Press is an imprint of the non-profit Hub City Writers Project, founded in 1995 to foster a sense of community through the literary arts. Our metaphor of organization purposely looks backward to the nineteenth century when Spartanburg was known as the "hub city," a place where railroads converged and departed.

Recent Hub City Nonfiction Titles
Outdoor Adventures in the Upcountry • Michel Stone, editor
Banjos, Barbecue and Boiled Peanuts • Kirk Neely
Artists Among Us • Ed Emory, editor, and Stephen Stinson, photographer
The Patron Saint of Dreams • Philip Gerard
Rockin' a Hard Place • John Jeter
Middlewood Journal • Helen Scott Correll